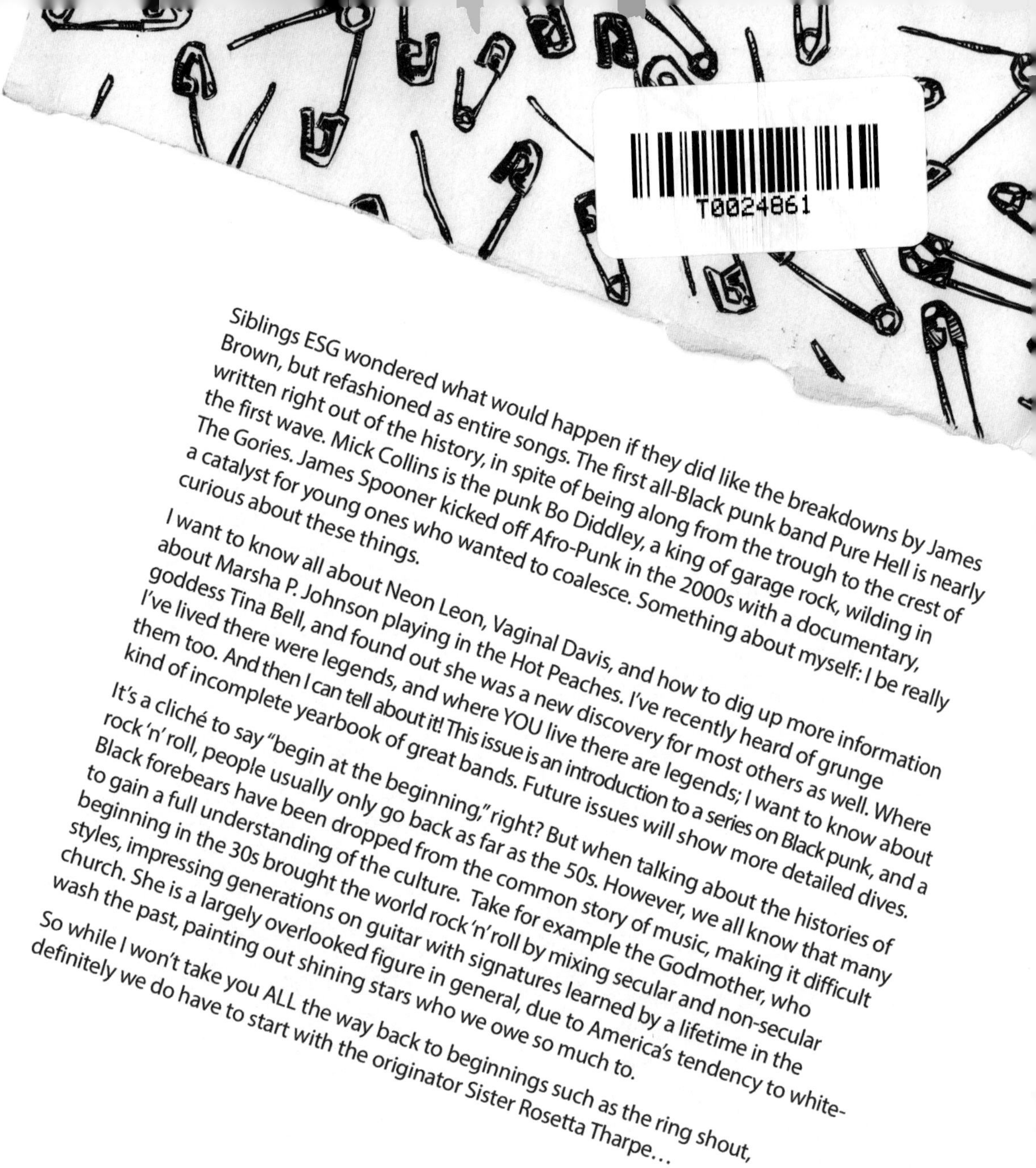

Siblings ESG wondered what would happen if they did like the breakdowns by James Brown, but refashioned as entire songs. The first all-Black punk band Pure Hell is nearly written right out of the history, in spite of being along from the trough to the crest of the first wave. Mick Collins is the punk Bo Diddley, a king of garage rock, wilding in The Gories. James Spooner kicked off Afro-Punk in the 2000s with a documentary, a catalyst for young ones who wanted to coalesce. Something about myself: I be really curious about these things.

I want to know all about Neon Leon, Vaginal Davis, and how to dig up more information about Marsha P. Johnson playing in the Hot Peaches. I've recently heard of grunge goddess Tina Bell, and found out she was a new discovery for most others as well. Where I've lived there were legends, and where YOU live there are legends; I want to know about them too. And then I can tell about it! This issue is an introduction to a series on Black punk, and a kind of incomplete yearbook of great bands. Future issues will show more detailed dives.

It's a cliché to say "begin at the beginning," right? But when talking about the histories of rock 'n' roll, people usually only go back as far as the 50s. However, we all know that many Black forebears have been dropped from the common story of music, making it difficult to gain a full understanding of the culture. Take for example the Godmother, who beginning in the 30s brought the world rock 'n' roll by mixing secular and non-secular styles, impressing generations on guitar with signatures learned by a lifetime in the church. She is a largely overlooked figure in general, due to America's tendency to white-wash the past, painting out shining stars who we owe so much to.

So while I won't take you ALL the way back to beginnings such as the ring shout, definitely we do have to start with the originator Sister Rosetta Tharpe…

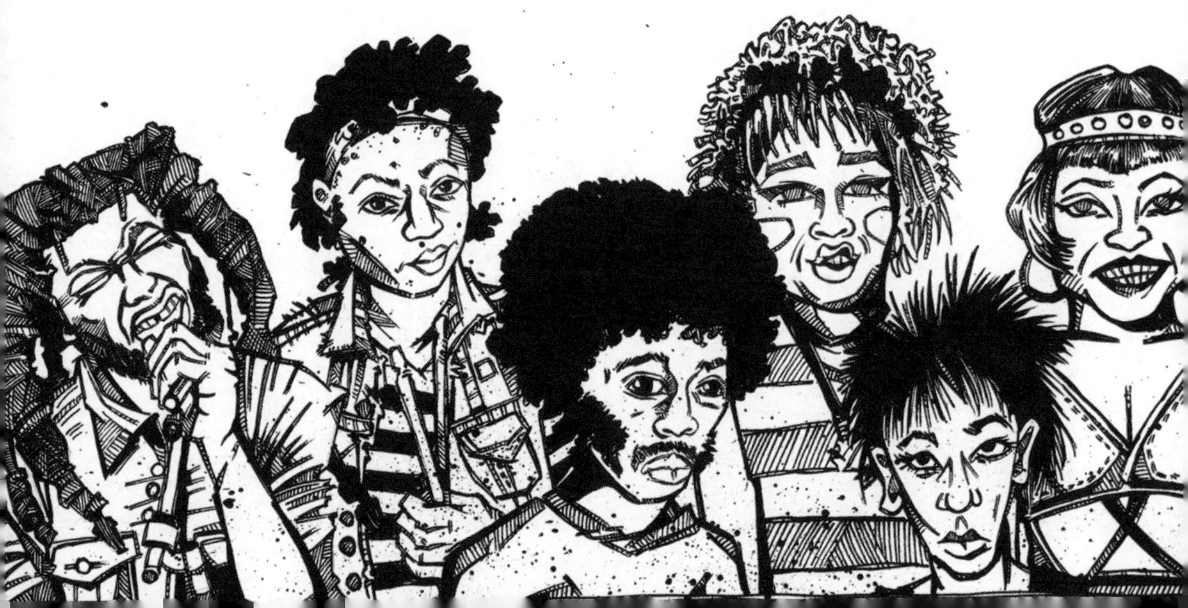

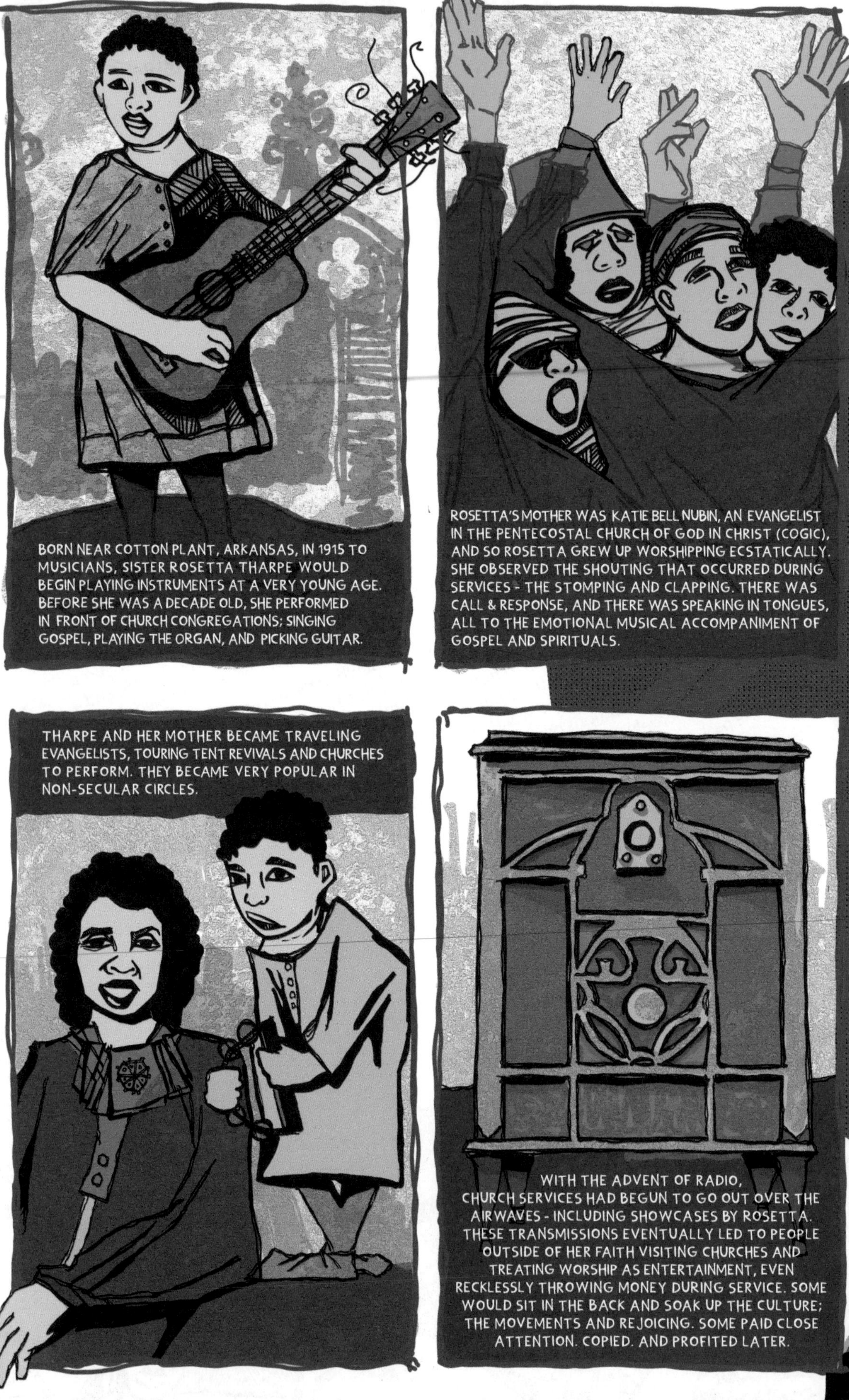
BORN NEAR COTTON PLANT, ARKANSAS, IN 1915 TO MUSICIANS, SISTER ROSETTA THARPE WOULD BEGIN PLAYING INSTRUMENTS AT A VERY YOUNG AGE. BEFORE SHE WAS A DECADE OLD, SHE PERFORMED IN FRONT OF CHURCH CONGREGATIONS; SINGING GOSPEL, PLAYING THE ORGAN, AND PICKING GUITAR.
ROSETTA'S MOTHER WAS KATIE BELL NUBIN, AN EVANGELIST IN THE PENTECOSTAL CHURCH OF GOD IN CHRIST (COGIC), AND SO ROSETTA GREW UP WORSHIPPING ECSTATICALLY. SHE OBSERVED THE SHOUTING THAT OCCURRED DURING SERVICES - THE STOMPING AND CLAPPING. THERE WAS CALL & RESPONSE, AND THERE WAS SPEAKING IN TONGUES, ALL TO THE EMOTIONAL MUSICAL ACCOMPANIMENT OF GOSPEL AND SPIRITUALS.
THARPE AND HER MOTHER BECAME TRAVELING EVANGELISTS, TOURING TENT REVIVALS AND CHURCHES TO PERFORM. THEY BECAME VERY POPULAR IN NON-SECULAR CIRCLES.
WITH THE ADVENT OF RADIO, CHURCH SERVICES HAD BEGUN TO GO OUT OVER THE AIRWAVES - INCLUDING SHOWCASES BY ROSETTA. THESE TRANSMISSIONS EVENTUALLY LED TO PEOPLE OUTSIDE OF HER FAITH VISITING CHURCHES AND TREATING WORSHIP AS ENTERTAINMENT, EVEN RECKLESSLY THROWING MONEY DURING SERVICE. SOME WOULD SIT IN THE BACK AND SOAK UP THE CULTURE; THE MOVEMENTS AND REJOICING. SOME PAID CLOSE ATTENTION. COPIED. AND PROFITED LATER.

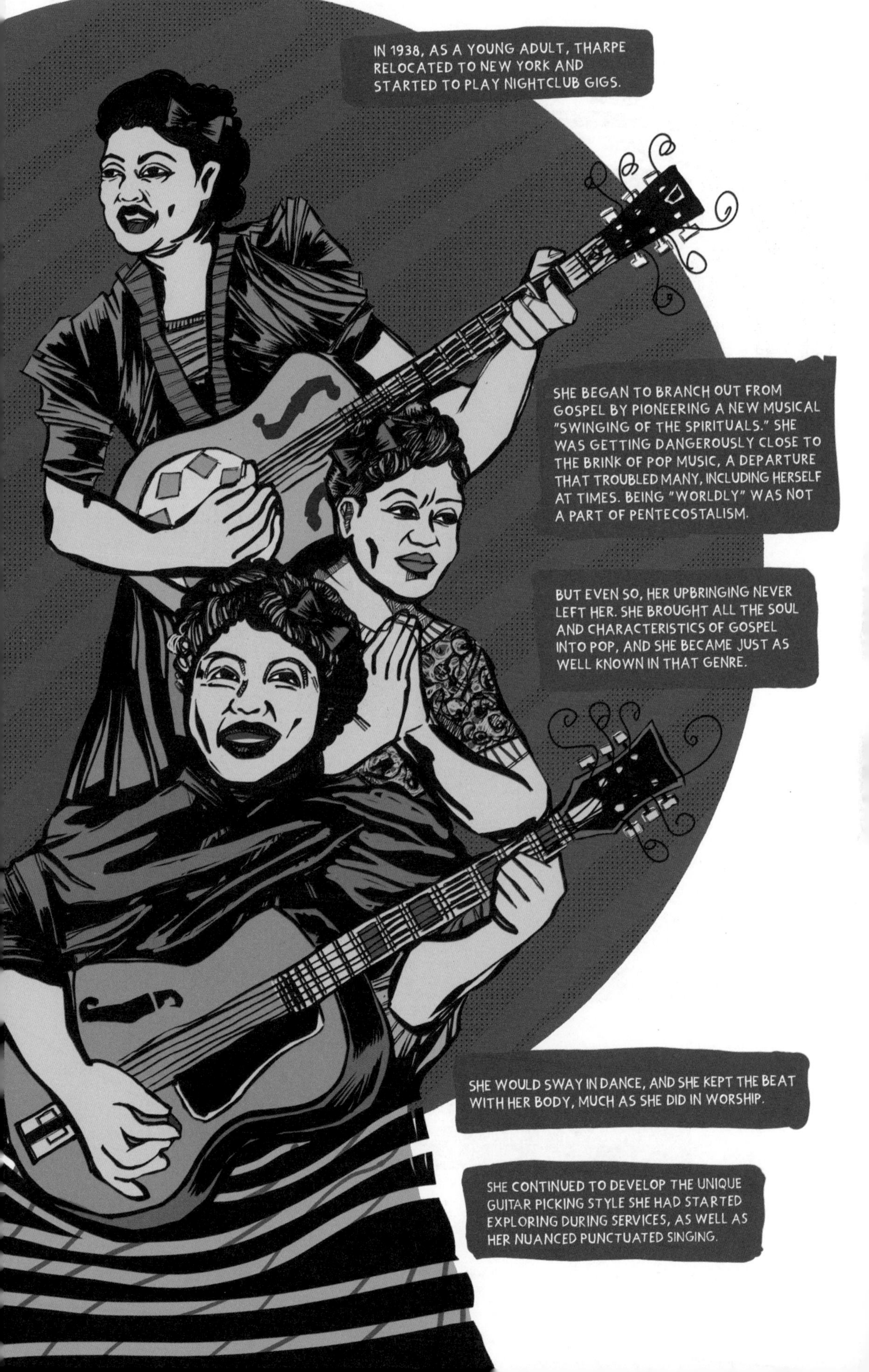
IN 1938, AS A YOUNG ADULT, THARPE RELOCATED TO NEW YORK AND STARTED TO PLAY NIGHTCLUB GIGS.
SHE BEGAN TO BRANCH OUT FROM GOSPEL BY PIONEERING A NEW MUSICAL "SWINGING OF THE SPIRITUALS." SHE WAS GETTING DANGEROUSLY CLOSE TO THE BRINK OF POP MUSIC, A DEPARTURE THAT TROUBLED MANY, INCLUDING HERSELF AT TIMES. BEING "WORLDLY" WAS NOT A PART OF PENTECOSTALISM.
BUT EVEN SO, HER UPBRINGING NEVER LEFT HER. SHE BROUGHT ALL THE SOUL AND CHARACTERISTICS OF GOSPEL INTO POP, AND SHE BECAME JUST AS WELL KNOWN IN THAT GENRE.
SHE WOULD SWAY IN DANCE, AND SHE KEPT THE BEAT WITH HER BODY, MUCH AS SHE DID IN WORSHIP.
SHE CONTINUED TO DEVELOP THE UNIQUE GUITAR PICKING STYLE SHE HAD STARTED EXPLORING DURING SERVICES, AS WELL AS HER NUANCED PUNCTUATED SINGING.

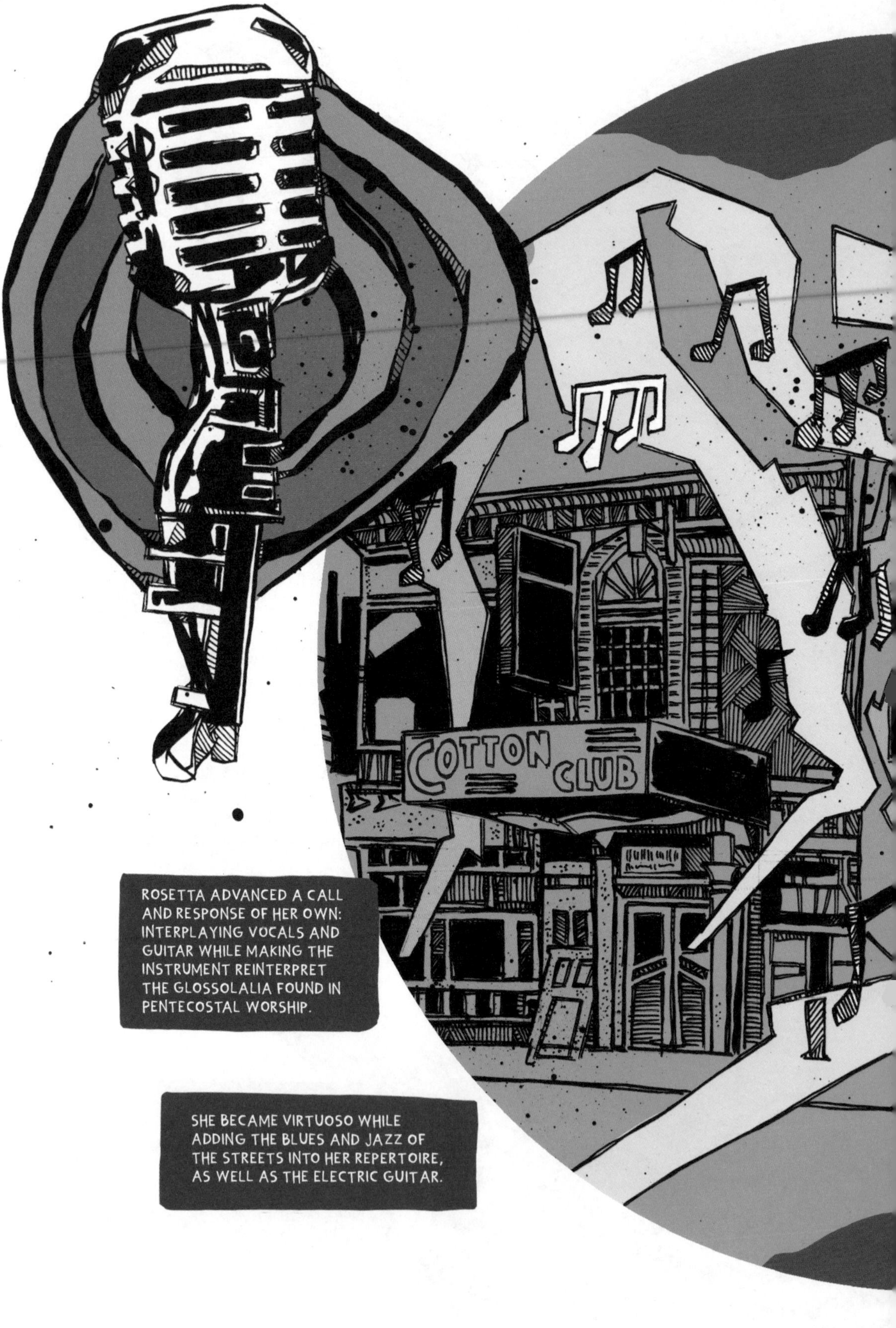
COTTON CLUB
ROSETTA ADVANCED A CALL AND RESPONSE OF HER OWN: INTERPLAYING VOCALS AND GUITAR WHILE MAKING THE INSTRUMENT REINTERPRET THE GLOSSOLALIA FOUND IN PENTECOSTAL WORSHIP.
SHE BECAME VIRTUOSO WHILE ADDING THE BLUES AND JAZZ OF THE STREETS INTO HER REPERTOIRE, AS WELL AS THE ELECTRIC GUITAR.

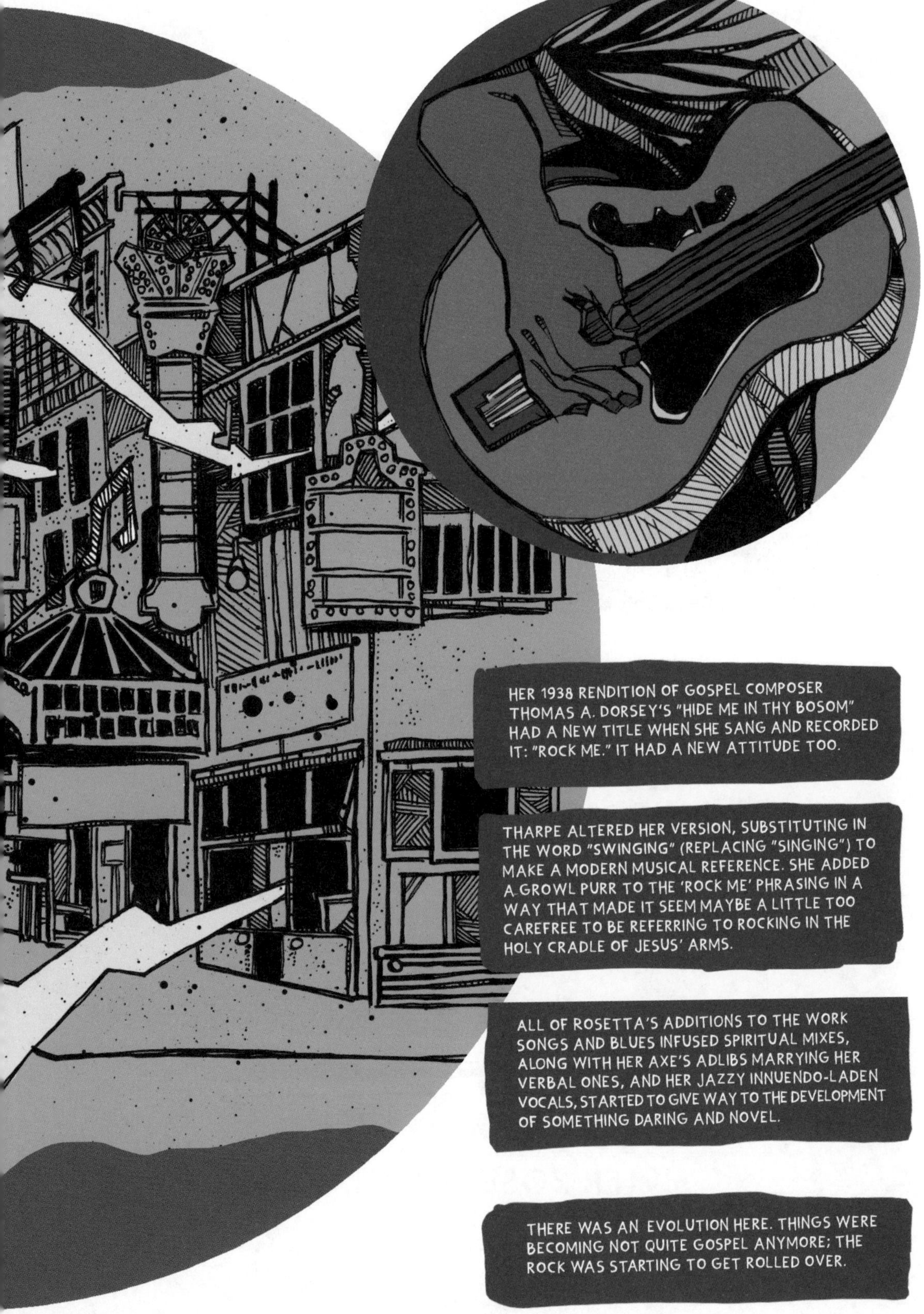
HER 1938 RENDITION OF GOSPEL COMPOSER THOMAS A. DORSEY'S "HIDE ME IN THY BOSOM" HAD A NEW TITLE WHEN SHE SANG AND RECORDED IT: "ROCK ME." IT HAD A NEW ATTITUDE TOO.
THARPE ALTERED HER VERSION, SUBSTITUTING IN THE WORD "SWINGING" (REPLACING "SINGING") TO MAKE A MODERN MUSICAL REFERENCE. SHE ADDED A GROWL PURR TO THE 'ROCK ME' PHRASING IN A WAY THAT MADE IT SEEM MAYBE A LITTLE TOO CAREFREE TO BE REFERRING TO ROCKING IN THE HOLY CRADLE OF JESUS' ARMS.
ALL OF ROSETTA'S ADDITIONS TO THE WORK SONGS AND BLUES INFUSED SPIRITUAL MIXES, ALONG WITH HER AXE'S ADLIBS MARRYING HER VERBAL ONES, AND HER JAZZY INNUENDO-LADEN VOCALS, STARTED TO GIVE WAY TO THE DEVELOPMENT OF SOMETHING DARING AND NOVEL.
THERE WAS AN EVOLUTION HERE. THINGS WERE BECOMING NOT QUITE GOSPEL ANYMORE; THE ROCK WAS STARTING TO GET ROLLED OVER.

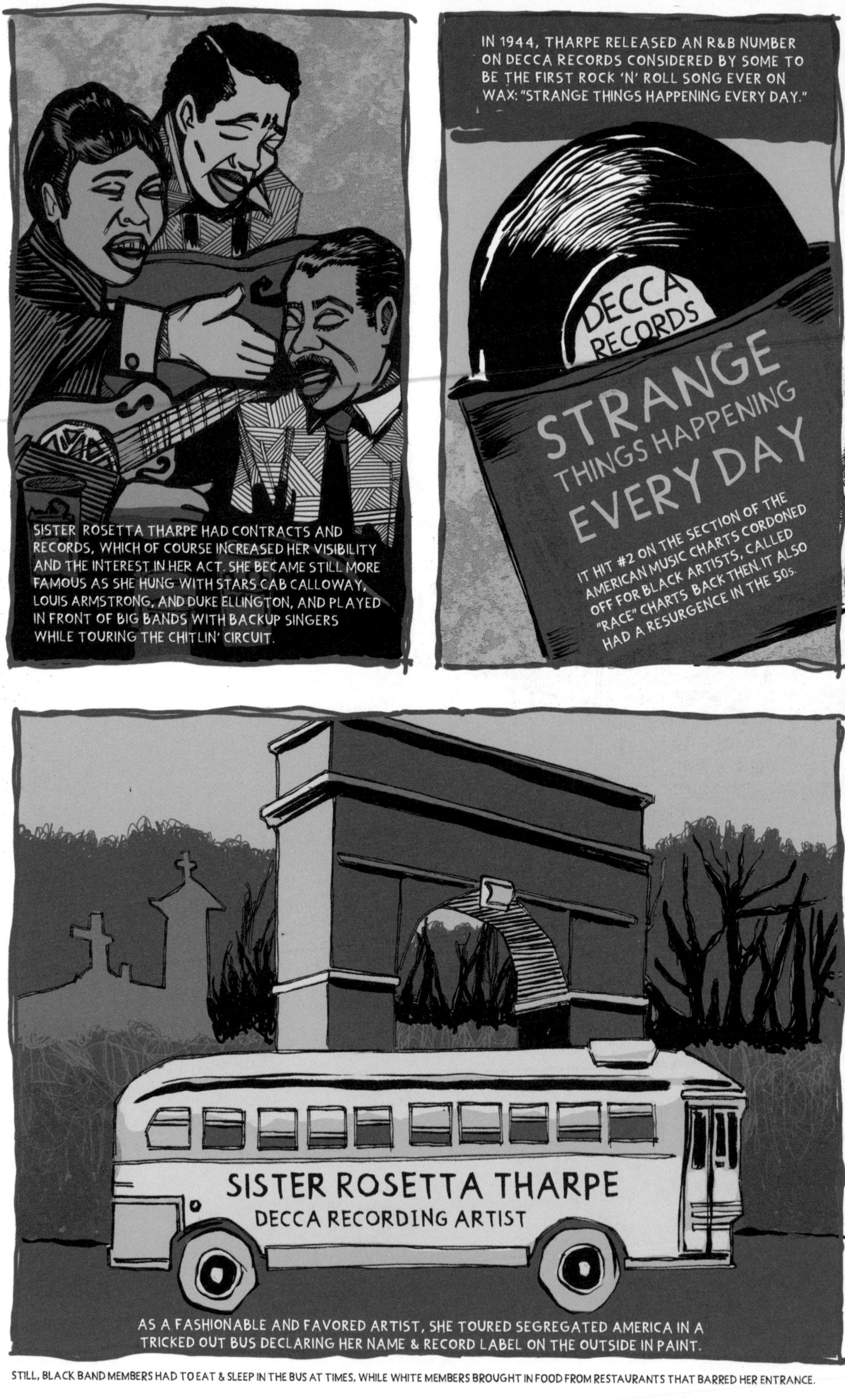
SISTER ROSETTA THARPE HAD CONTRACTS AND RECORDS, WHICH OF COURSE INCREASED HER VISIBILITY AND THE INTEREST IN HER ACT. SHE BECAME STILL MORE FAMOUS AS SHE HUNG WITH STARS CAB CALLOWAY, LOUIS ARMSTRONG, AND DUKE ELLINGTON, AND PLAYED IN FRONT OF BIG BANDS WITH BACKUP SINGERS WHILE TOURING THE CHITLIN' CIRCUIT.
IN 1944, THARPE RELEASED AN R&B NUMBER ON DECCA RECORDS CONSIDERED BY SOME TO BE THE FIRST ROCK 'N' ROLL SONG EVER ON WAX: "STRANGE THINGS HAPPENING EVERY DAY."
DECCA RECORDS
STRANGE THINGS HAPPENING EVERY DAY
IT HIT #2 ON THE SECTION OF THE AMERICAN MUSIC CHARTS CORDONED OFF FOR BLACK ARTISTS, CALLED "RACE" CHARTS BACK THEN. IT ALSO HAD A RESURGENCE IN THE 50s.
SISTER ROSETTA THARPE
DECCA RECORDING ARTIST
AS A FASHIONABLE AND FAVORED ARTIST, SHE TOURED SEGREGATED AMERICA IN A TRICKED OUT BUS DECLARING HER NAME & RECORD LABEL ON THE OUTSIDE IN PAINT.

STILL, BLACK BAND MEMBERS HAD TO EAT & SLEEP IN THE BUS AT TIMES, WHILE WHITE MEMBERS BROUGHT IN FOOD FROM RESTAURANTS THAT BARRED HER ENTRANCE.

SISTER ROSETTA THARPE TRAVELED TO MANY AMERICAN CITIES TO PERFORM. SHE VISITED CANADA, AND HAD EUROPEAN AND SCANDINAVIAN TOURS, STARTING IN THE 50s: GRACING ENGLAND, SCOTLAND, FRANCE, MONTE CARLO, GERMANY, DENMARK, SWEDEN, AND AS WELL SWITZERLAND. SHE APPEARED ON TV SHOWS AND OVER RADIO, RELEASED RECORDS, PUT ON SIZEABLE SHOWS AND WAS FEATURED IN THE PRESS. SHE PERFORMED OUTRAGEOUS AND WIDELY CELEBRATED PUBLICITY STUNTS. HER POPULARITY DID WANE, BUT FIRST HER REACH WENT FAR.

IF THE START OF ROCK 'N' ROLL RESIDES IN THE PERSON WHO LIT THE FLAME, THEN IT WAS SISTER ROSETTA THARPE BY MANY YEARS AND ALL MEANS. SHE EVEN CONSIDERED HERSELF THE GENESIS, NOTING A THREAD THAT RAN THROUGH GOSPEL TO ROCK 'N' ROLL, WITH PIT STOPS AT BLUES, REVIVAL, AND JAZZ ALONG THE WAY. CHUCK BERRY, LITTLE RICHARD, ETTA JAMES, ARETHA FRANKLIN, TINA TURNER AND MANY OTHERS (INCLUDING HE WHO WILL REMAIN UNNAMED), JOHNNY CASH, JERRY LEE LEWIS, THEY ALL CITE HER AS A BELOVED INFLUENCE.

HOWEVER HER ROLE IS STILL VASTLY UNKNOWN, UNSUNG, OR TREATED AS A CUTE TALE THAT BLACK PEOPLE KEEP ALIVE TO COMFORT THEMSELVES WITH. BLACK PEOPLE ARE WRITTEN OUT OF HISTORY EASILY AND FREQUENTLY AND THAT IS WHY IT'S IMPORTANT FOR US TO REMAIN DILIGENT IN KEEPING TRUTHS ALIVE.

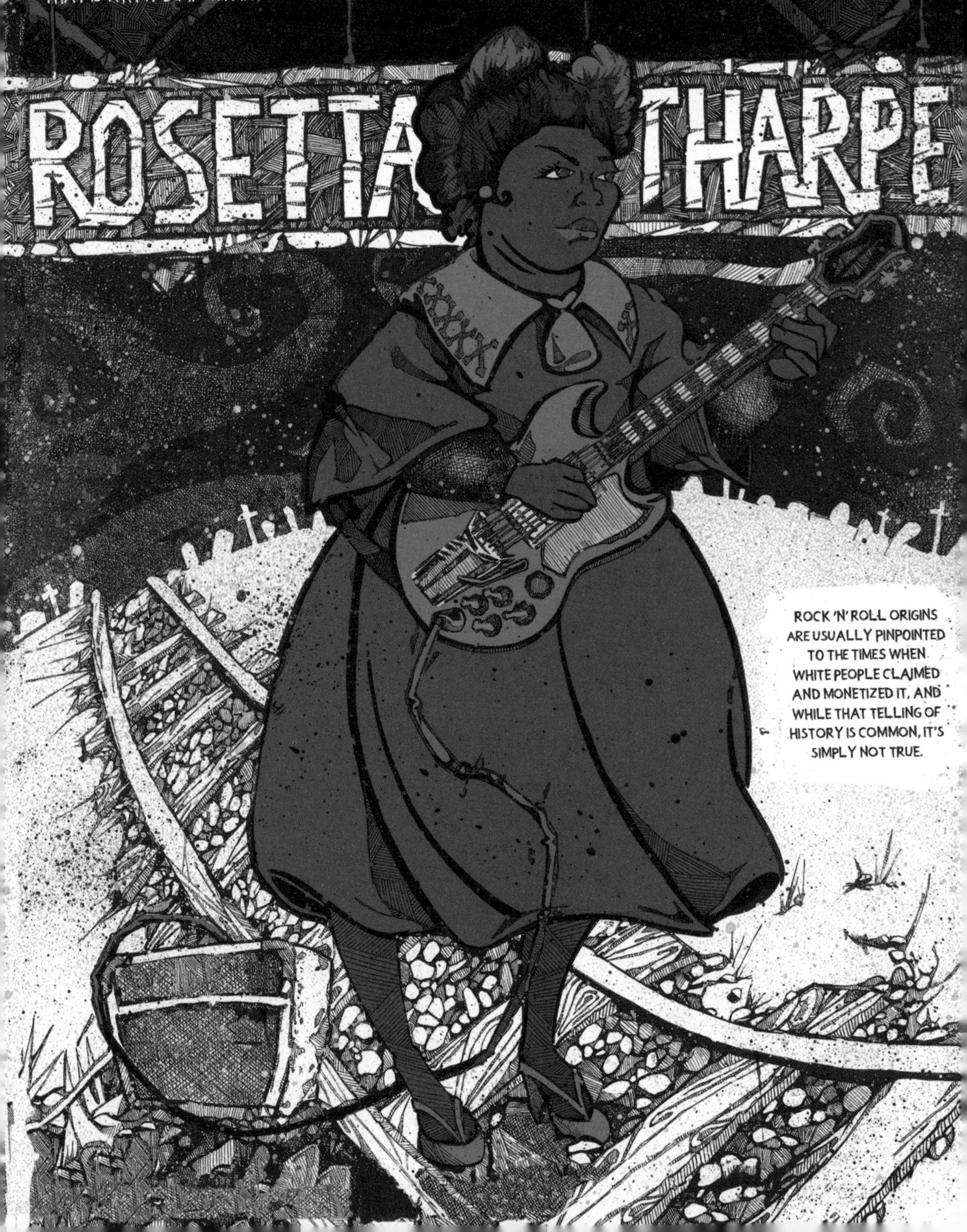
ROSETTA THARPE
ROCK 'N' ROLL ORIGINS ARE USUALLY PINPOINTED TO THE TIMES WHEN WHITE PEOPLE CLAIMED AND MONETIZED IT, AND WHILE THAT TELLING OF HISTORY IS COMMON, IT'S SIMPLY NOT TRUE.

PROTO PUNK

DETROIT

1973

THOUGH THE BROTHERS HACKNEY HAD BEGUN PLAYING AS A BAND IN 1971, IN 1973 THEY SWITCHED FROM THE FUNK-BASED SOUND THAT THEY HAD BEEN USING TO A ROCK-BASED SOUND. THEY BEGAN GOING BY THE NAME "DEATH" IN '74.

THIS TIGHTKNIT PROTOPUNK BAND CREATED THEIR OWN MYTHOLOGY AND THEIR OWN RULES, REBELLING AGAINST WHAT THE WORLD (AND THE NEIGHBORHOOD) TOLD THEM WAS ACCEPTABLE FOR A BAND OF BLACK MEN TO BE.

DAVID HACKNEY WAS THE IMAGINATIVE LEADER, CULTIVATING SOUND AND IMAGERY INTO SOLID CREED.

THE ONLY PROBLEM THEN WAS THAT THE WORLD, FOR A TIME, DECIDED NOT TO PLAY ALONG.

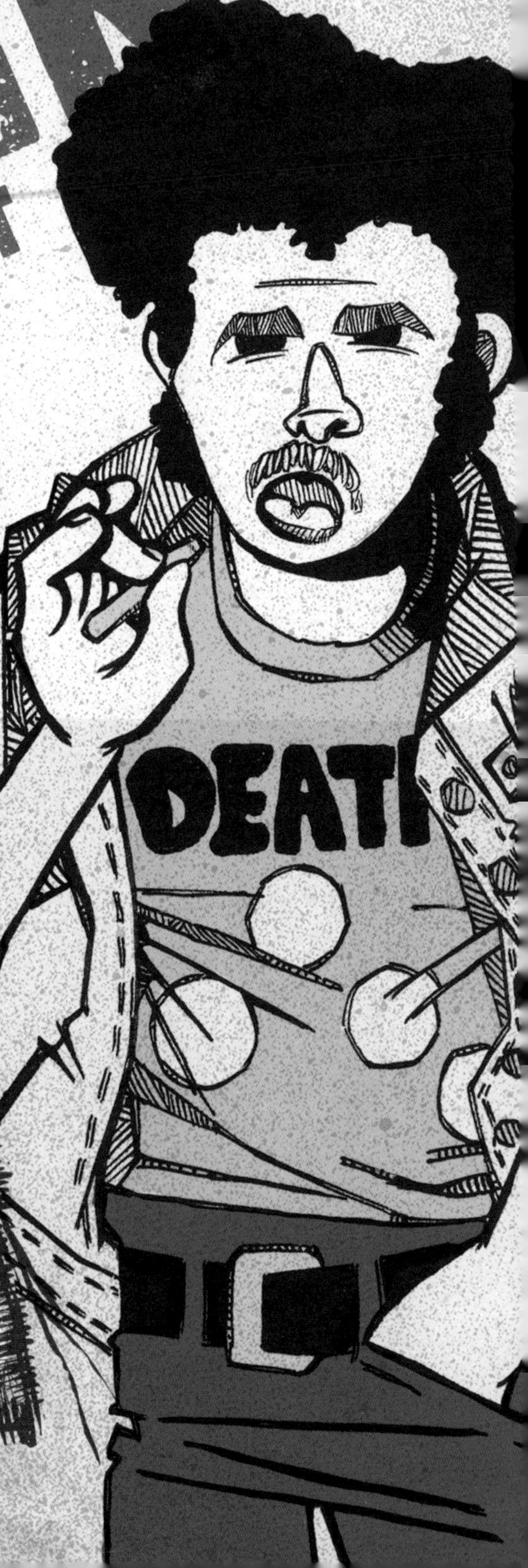

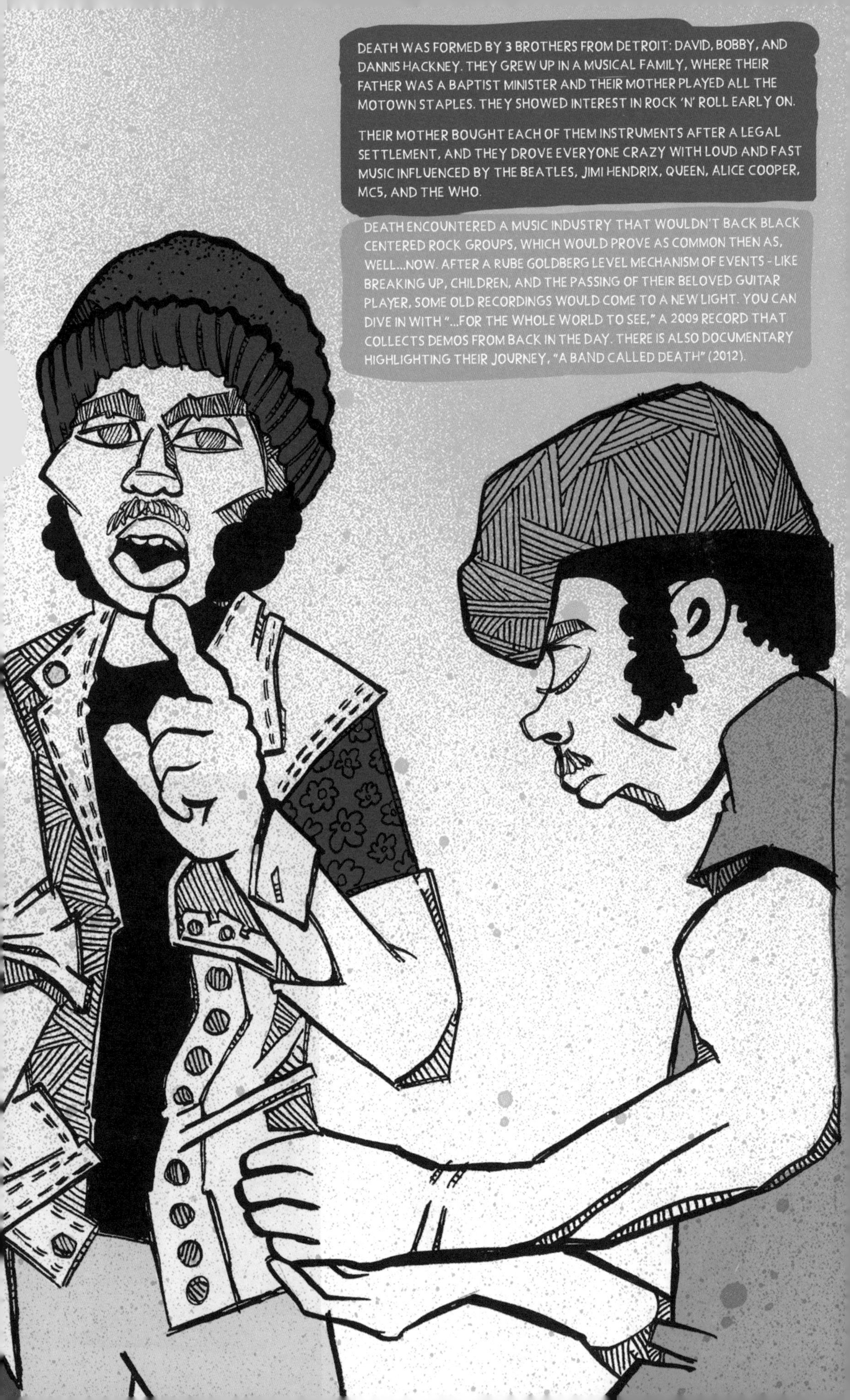
DEATH WAS FORMED BY 3 BROTHERS FROM DETROIT: DAVID, BOBBY, AND DANNIS HACKNEY. THEY GREW UP IN A MUSICAL FAMILY, WHERE THEIR FATHER WAS A BAPTIST MINISTER AND THEIR MOTHER PLAYED ALL THE MOTOWN STAPLES. THEY SHOWED INTEREST IN ROCK 'N' ROLL EARLY ON.
THEIR MOTHER BOUGHT EACH OF THEM INSTRUMENTS AFTER A LEGAL SETTLEMENT, AND THEY DROVE EVERYONE CRAZY WITH LOUD AND FAST MUSIC INFLUENCED BY THE BEATLES, JIMI HENDRIX, QUEEN, ALICE COOPER, MC5, AND THE WHO.
DEATH ENCOUNTERED A MUSIC INDUSTRY THAT WOULDN'T BACK BLACK CENTERED ROCK GROUPS, WHICH WOULD PROVE AS COMMON THEN AS, WELL...NOW. AFTER A RUBE GOLDBERG LEVEL MECHANISM OF EVENTS - LIKE BREAKING UP, CHILDREN, AND THE PASSING OF THEIR BELOVED GUITAR PLAYER, SOME OLD RECORDINGS WOULD COME TO A NEW LIGHT. YOU CAN DIVE IN WITH "...FOR THE WHOLE WORLD TO SEE," A 2009 RECORD THAT COLLECTS DEMOS FROM BACK IN THE DAY. THERE IS ALSO DOCUMENTARY HIGHLIGHTING THEIR JOURNEY, "A BAND CALLED DEATH" (2012).

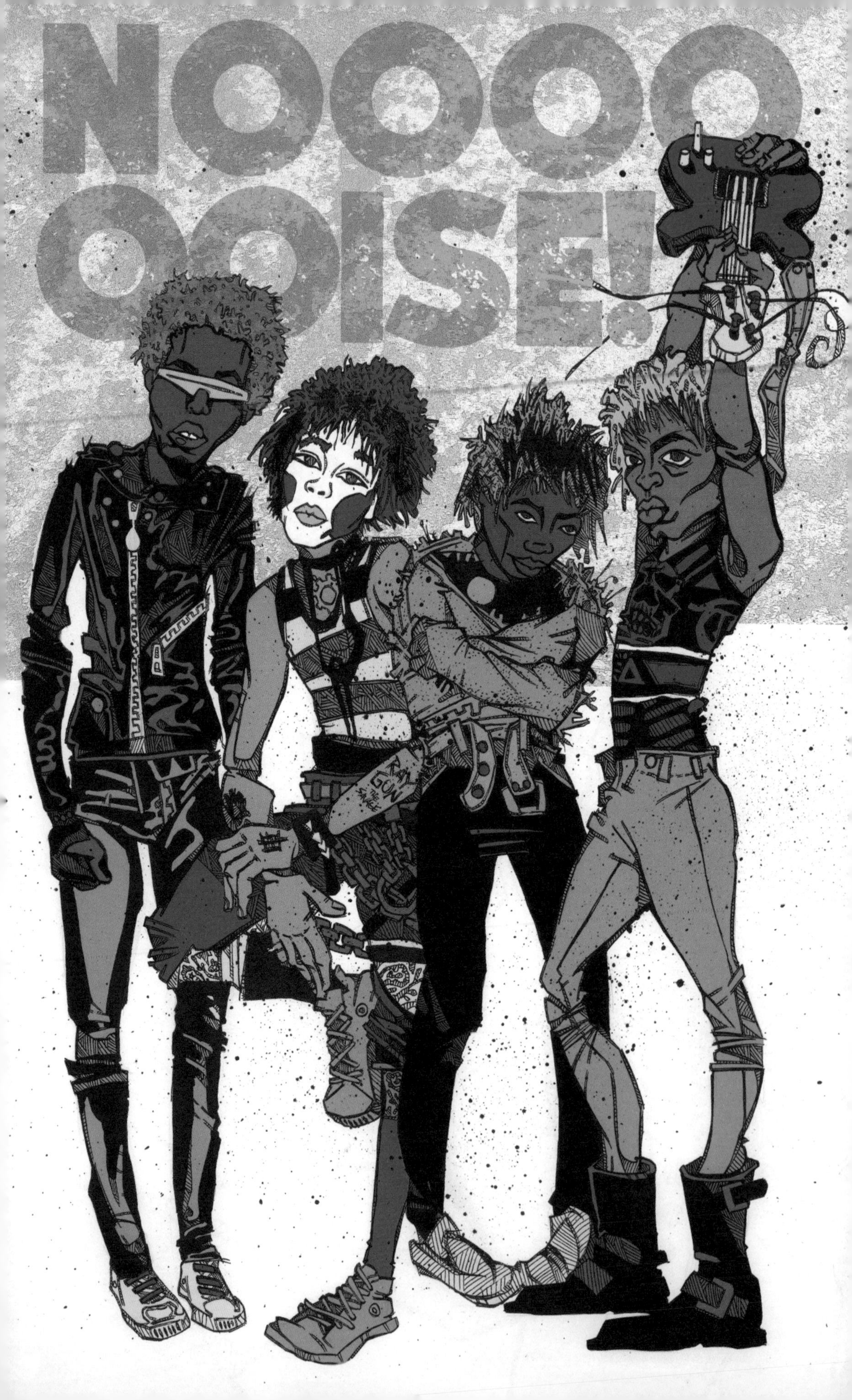
NOOOO
OOISE!
RAY GUN THE SAVAGE

1974 NEW YORK
WEST PHILLY

PURE HELL

"WE WERE REALLY REALLY REALLY OUT THERE MAN... WALKING FROM 59TH AND ADDISON TO SPRUCE TO CATCH THE BUS THROUGH GANG TERRITORY WITH HIGH HEELS AND A WIG ON."

– LENNY BOLES

Pure Hell documentary, Woodshop Films

KENNY "STINKER" GORDON: VOCALS
MICHAEL "SPIDER" SANDERS: DRUMS
LENNY "STEEL" BOLES: BASS
PRESTON "CHIPWRECK" MORRIS: GUITAR

MEETING IN THEIR HOMETOWN OF WEST PHILADELPHIA AND BONDING OVER LOVE OF ROCK, PSYCHEDELIC, ACID, & PROTOPUNK LIKE HENDRIX, SLY AND THE FAMILY STONE, IGGY POP, AND MC5, THE BAND FIRST DUBBED "PRETTY POISON" BECAME PURE HELL IN 1974 AND SHOT OVER TO NEW YORK AFTER READING MAGAZINES DETAILING THE SCENE, AND BECOMING FANS OF THE NEW YORK DOLLS. THE DOLLS WOULD SOON BECOME THEIR FRIENDS AND GIGMATES, PUTTING PURE HELL UP IN THEIR CHELSEA LOFT FOR A BIT. THEY ALSO RAN WITH SID VICIOUS (SEX PISTOLS) AND HIS GIRLFRIEND/MANAGER NANCY SPUNGEON. THEY OPENED FOR SID'S SOLO ACT DURING HIS NEW YORK RESIDENCY, BEFORE LEAVING FOR THEIR FIRST EUROPEAN TOUR. SOON AFTER THAT, NANCY DIED, AND HER PASSING WAS SO HIGHLY SENSATIONALIZED THAT IT CAUSED MORE PUBLICITY FOR PURE HELL BECAUSE OF THEIR PROXIMITY TO THE TRAGEDY.

AT FIRST PURE HELL LIVED IN THE INFAMOUS CHELSEA HOTEL AND PLAYED THE REGULAR NEW YORK VENUES: MOTHER'S, THE HIPPODROME, AND MAX'S KANSAS CITY. PURE HELL WENT WILD ON THEIR EQUIPMENT, AND THEY PREDATED HARDCORE WITH THEIR FAST ATTACK AND ASSAULT METHOD ON INSTRUMENTS. THEY RELEASED A SINGLE (A VERSION OF "THESE BOOTS ARE MADE FOR WALKING" BY NANCY SINATRA) IN EUROPE THAT WENT TOP FIVE ON THE UK ALTERNATIVE CHARTS, BUT THEN THEY HAD A SEVERE FALLING OUT WITH A MANAGER, HALTING A LOT OF THEIR PROGRESS. AT THE SAME TIME THEY BATTLED A DOUBLE-EDGE SWORD OF RACISM: IGNORED BY THE ROCK LABELS THAT PUT OUT THEIR PUNK PEERS, THEY WERE ENCOURAGED BY OTHER LABELS TO CONFORM TO "BLACK GENRES" IN ORDER TO BE SIGNED. BUT THEY ENJOYED WHO THEY WERE AND WHAT THEY CREATED, AND STOOD STRONG. IN THE 80s, FACING AN ABRUPT CHANGE IN MUSICAL CLIMATE AND WORN OUT BY THE LIFESTYLE, THEY FELL APART.

YEARS LATER, WELFARE RECORDS WOULD RELEASE A FULL LENGTH ALBUM OF THE OLD RECORDINGS, SOME OF WHICH WERE RECOVERED FROM AN AUCTION SALE. NOISE ADDICTION CAME OUT IN 2006 WITH 15 TRACKS ON WAX. THERE IS ALSO A 7 INCH FLOATING AROUND THAT HENRY ROLLINS PUT OUT FOR A 2017 RECORD STORE DAY. THEY'VE GOTTEN TOGETHER SPORADICALLY OVER THE YEARS TO PLAY FESTIVALS AND SHOWS.

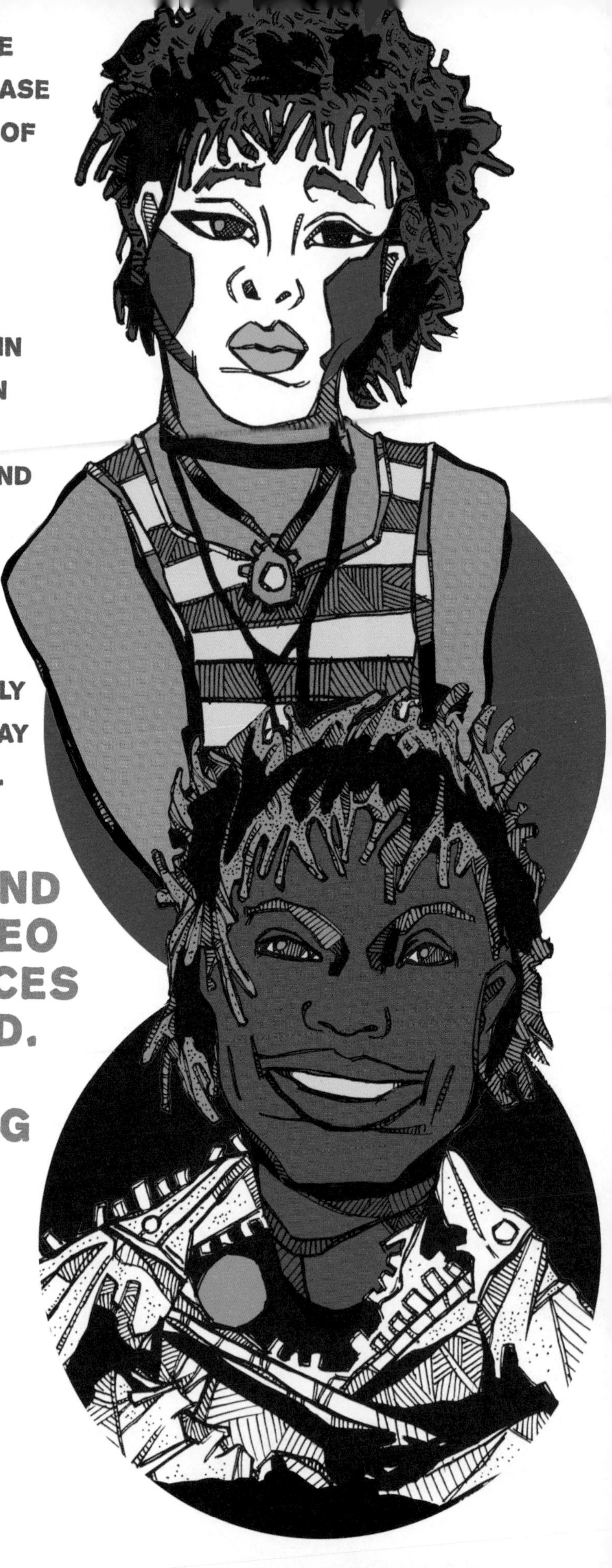

GO ONLINE AND LOOK UP VIDEO PERFORMANCES OF THIS BAND. I FEEL SO PROUD SEEING THEM PLAY. IT REALLY ANNOYS ME THAT I GREW UP NOT KNOWING ABOUT PURE HELL.

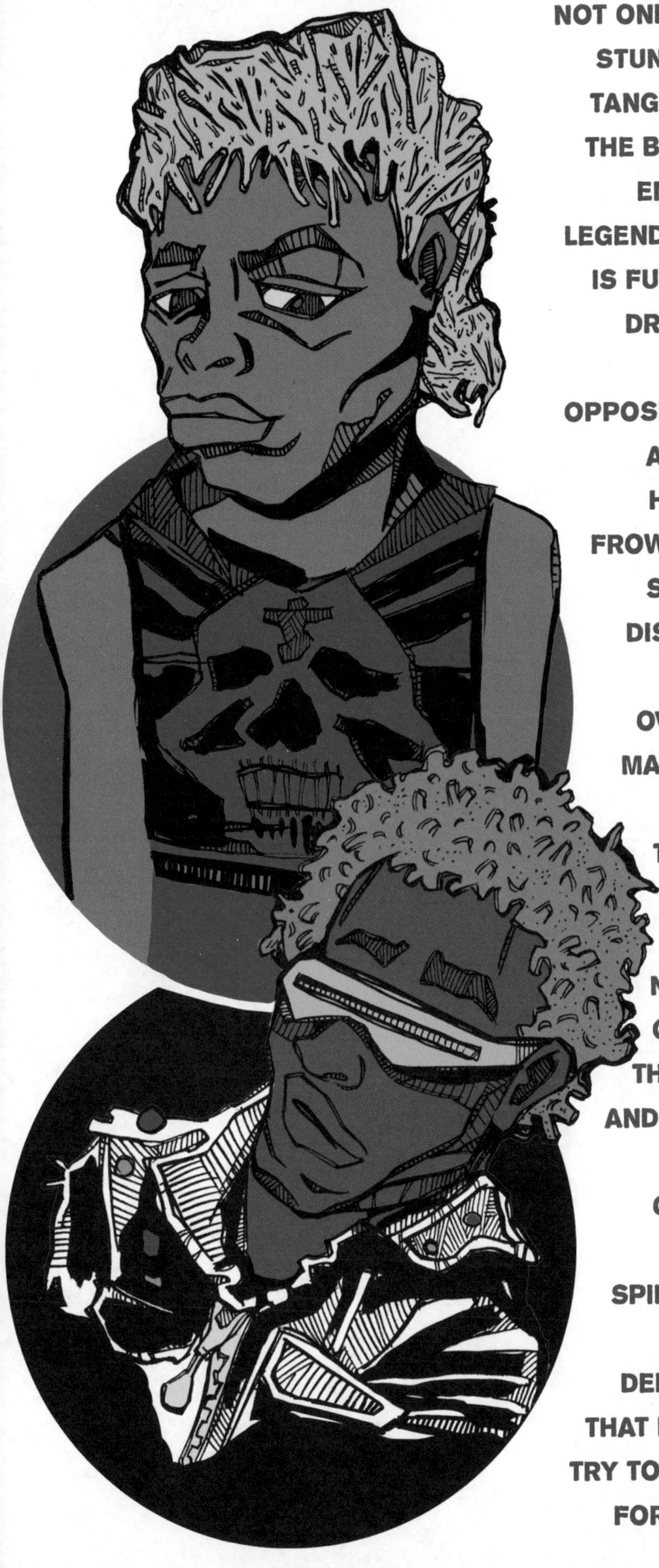

NOT ONLY ARE THEY REALLY STUNNING, THEIR TALE IS TANGLED UP WITH ALL OF THE BANDS THAT BECAME ENTRENCHED IN PUNK LEGEND. THEIR OWN STORY IS FULL OF DANGER, SEX, DRUGS, ROCK 'N' ROLL, CONTRADICTIONS, OPPOSITION AND INTRIGUE, ALL THAT STUFF. YOU HAVE TO PICTURE ME FROWNING, SIGHING, AND SHAKING MY HEAD IN DISGUST WHEN I THINK ABOUT THEM BEING OVERLOOKED. LIKE, IF I MADE WILDLY FICTIONAL MOVIES BASED ON TRUE LIFE YOU COULD CALL ME ALEX COX, I'D BE "SID AND NANCYING" THE FUCK OUT OF THEIR STORY. THIS IS LIVING HISTORY, AND I REALLY HOPE THAT THEY GET SOME OF THEIR DUE IN THIS LIFETIME. DRUMMER SPIDER PASSED IN 2002, RIP TO HIM. THIS IS DEF ONE OF THE BANDS THAT I'M MOST EXCITED TO TRY TO LEARN MORE ABOUT FOR THIS COMIC SERIES.

YOUNG PUNX WHO WANT TO STICK IT TOGETHER

1976

POLY STYRENE'S CALL TO ACTION IN BRITISH MUSIC WEEKLIES NME AND MELODY MAKER WAS THE START, AS SHE SWITCHED FROM HER REGGAE BEGINNINGS TO PUNK AFTER SEEING THE SEX PISTOLS LIVE. SHE FORMED X-RAY SPEX, RECRUITING HER ORIGINAL LINEUP IN 1976 LONDON.

MARIANNE JOAN ELLIOTT-SAID
THE BRITISH-SOMALIAN
PLASTIC POP DREAM
A TECHNICOLOR ECCENTRIC
FROM THE FIRST WAVE
OF PUNK ROCK

DRILLING WITH ATONAL SHRIEKS
PUNCTUATED DAGGERS
ANTI-CONSUMERISM AND
ENVIRONMENTAL CONCERNS
CREATING GLARINGLY BRIGHT
DYSTOPIAN MUSIC COMEDIES IN
DAYGLO WHILE SUBVERTING STYLISTIC
EXPECTATIONS BY SIMPLY APPEARING
AS HER PERSONA WOULD PREFER

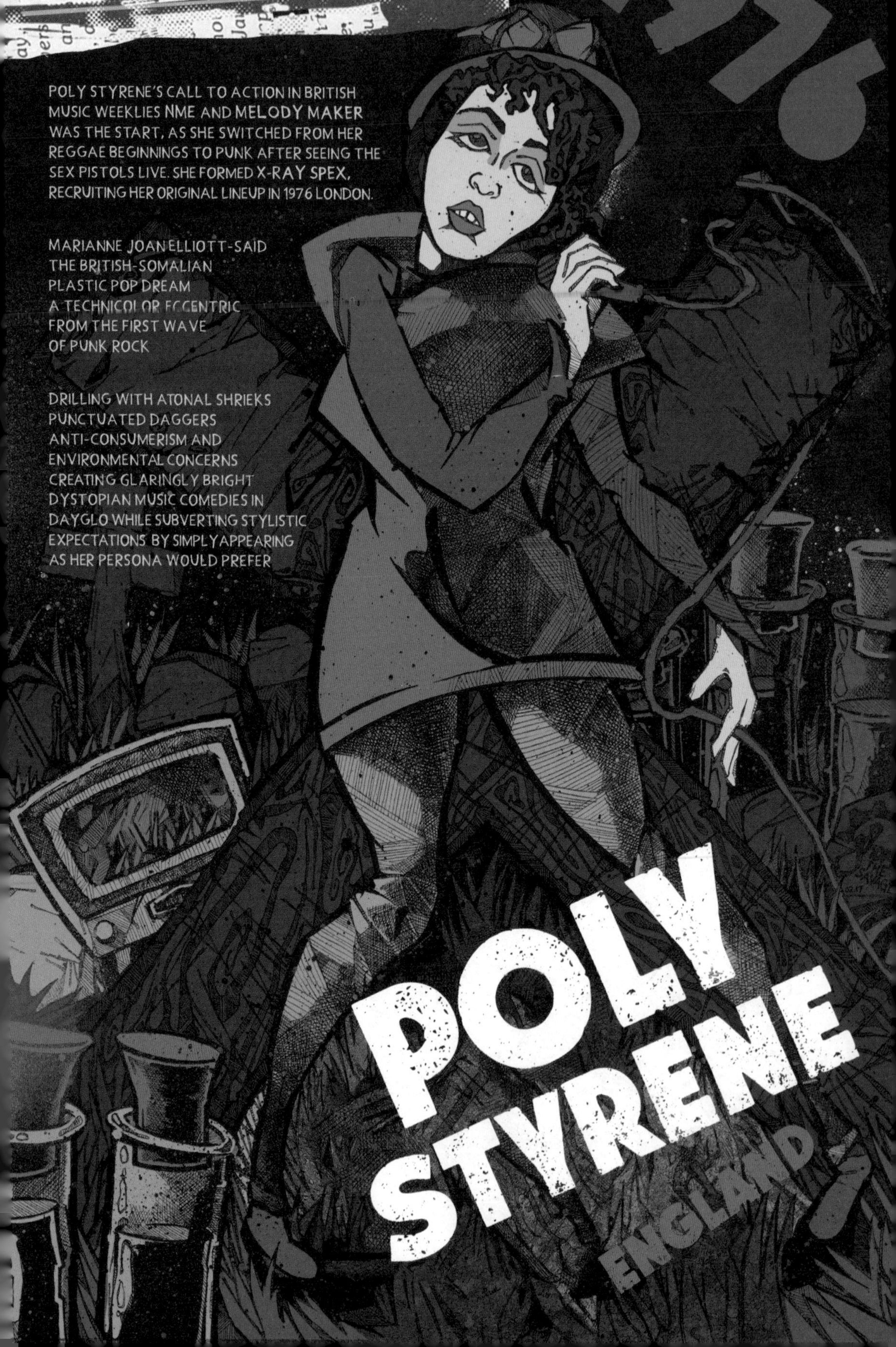

POLY STYRENE

ENGLAND

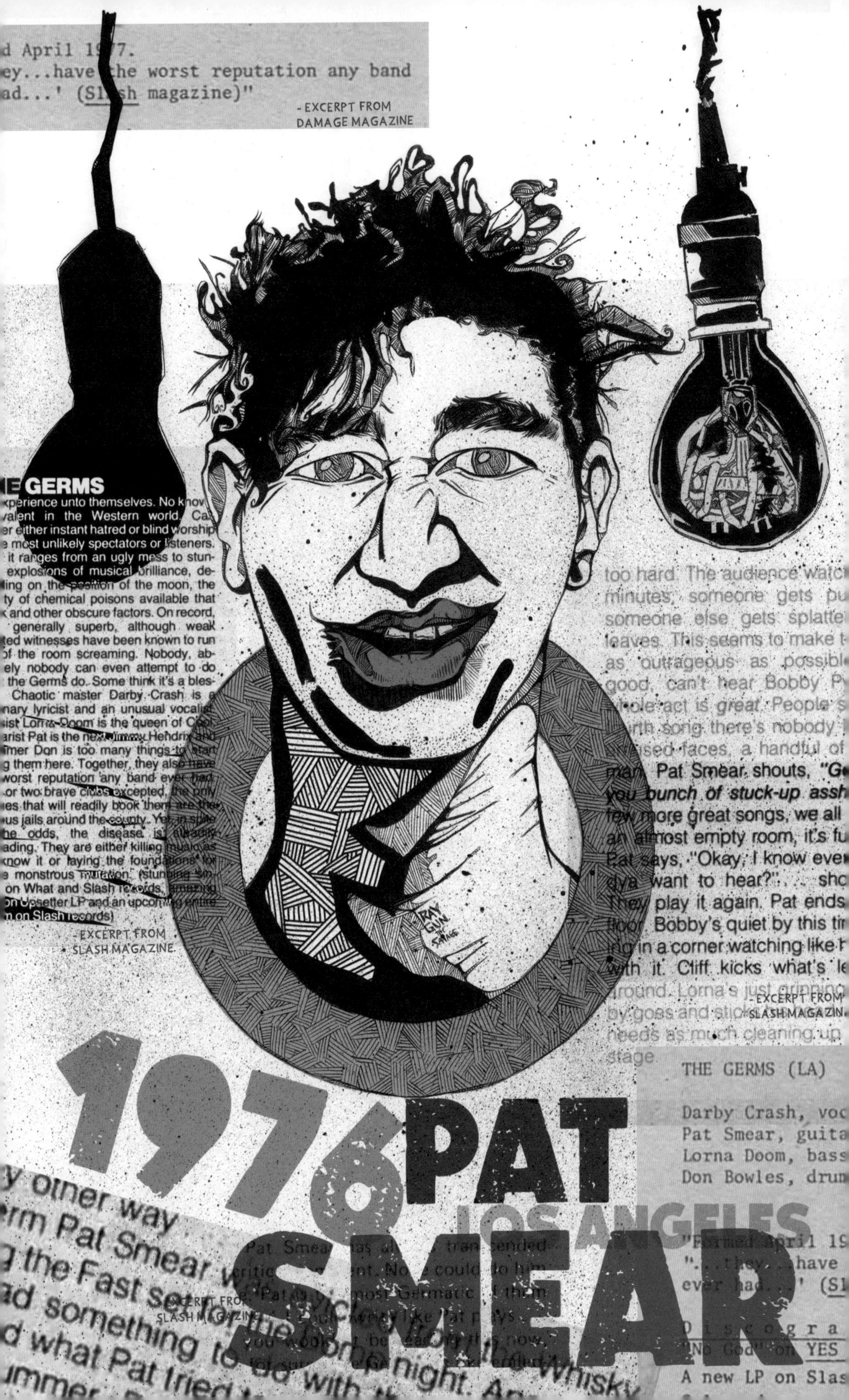

d April 1977.
ey...have the worst reputation any band
ad...' (Slash magazine)"
- EXCERPT FROM
DAMAGE MAGAZINE
E GERMS
xperience unto themselves. No know
valent in the Western world. Ca
er either instant hatred or blind worship
e most unlikely spectators or listeners.
it ranges from an ugly mess to stun-
explosions of musical brilliance, de-
ding on the position of the moon, the
ty of chemical poisons available that
k and other obscure factors. On record,
generally superb, although weak
ted witnesses have been known to run
of the room screaming. Nobody, ab-
ely nobody can even attempt to do
the Germs do. Some think it's a bles-
Chaotic master Darby Crash is a
nary lyricist and an unusual vocalist
sist Lorna Doom is the queen of Cool
arist Pat is the next Jimmy Hendrix and
mer Don is too many things to start
g them here. Together, they also have
worst reputation any band ever had.
or two brave clubs excepted, the only
es that will readily book them are the
us jails around the county. Yet in spite
he odds, the disease is already
ading. They are either killing music as
now it or laying the foundations for
e monstrous mutation. (stunning sin-
on What and Slash records, amazing
n Upsetter LP and an upcoming entire
n on Slash records)
- EXCERPT FROM
SLASH MAGAZINE
too hard. The audience watc
minutes, someone gets pu
someone else gets splatte
leaves. This seems to make t
as outrageous as possibl
good, can't hear Bobby P
whole act is great. People s
fourth song there's nobody
bruised faces, a handful of
man. Pat Smear shouts, "Ge
you bunch of stuck-up assh
few more great songs, we all
an almost empty room, it's fu
Pat says, "Okay, I know eve
dya want to hear?" ... sho
They play it again. Pat ends
floor. Bobby's quiet by this tir
ing in a corner watching like h
with it. Cliff kicks what's le
around. Lorna's just grinning
by goes and sticks
needs as much cleaning up
stage.
- EXCERPT FROM
SLASH MAGAZIN
THE GERMS (LA)
Darby Crash, voc
Pat Smear, guita
Lorna Doom, bass
Don Bowles, drum
"Formed April 19
"...they...have
ever had...' (Sl
D i s c o g r a
"No God" on YES
A new LP on Slas
RAY GUN THE SAVAGE
1976
PAT SMEAR
LOS ANGELES
y other way
erm Pat Smear
g the Fast set
ad something
d what Pat tried
ummer
Pat Smear has al transcended
criti ment. No could do him
Pat is the most Germatic of them
you would be reading this now
- EXCERPT FROM
SLASH MAGAZINE

"PUNK IS NOT MOHAWKS & SAFETY PINS IT'S AN ATTITUDE & A SPIRIT WITH A LINEAGE & A TRADITION"

-DON LETTS

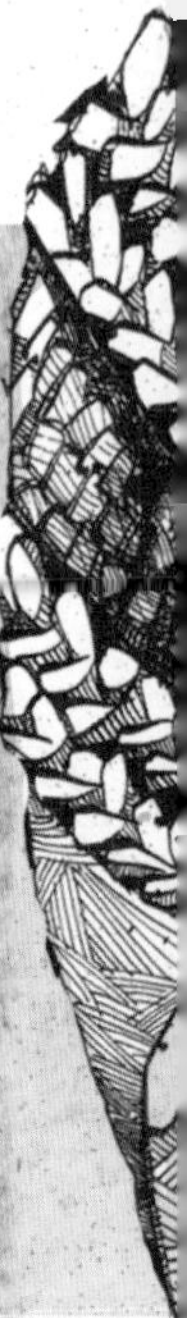

DON LETTS IS A DJ, MUSICIAN, AND FILMMAKER. HE INTRODUCED REGGAE MUSIC TO THE NASCENT BRITISH PUNK SCENE IN '75 BY PERMEATING THE AIR WITH DUB WHILE WORKING AT ACME ATTRACTIONS ON KINGS ROAD. HE SPUN REGGAE RECORDS IN BETWEEN SETS AT PUNK GIGS AT THE ROXY, WITH MAJOR IMPACT. HE WAS IN THE BANDS BIG AUDIO DYNAMITE AND SCREAMING TARGET, AND HE ALSO MANAGED THE POST-PUNK GROUP THE SLITS.

HIS FIRST FILM WAS THE PUNK ROCK MOVIE, SHOT IN 1977, AND HE WENT ON TO CREATE HUNDREDS OF MUSIC VIDEOS (INCLUDING SEVERAL FOR THE CLASH), ALONG WITH MANY DOCUMENTARIES. HE DID SUN RA: THE BROTHER FROM ANOTHER PLANET (2005), PUNK: ATTITUDE (2005), THE STORY OF SKINHEAD (2016), AND THE CLASH: WESTWAY TO THE WORLD (2000). HE CURRENTLY HOSTS WEEKLY SHOW CULTURE CLASH RADIO ON THE BBC.

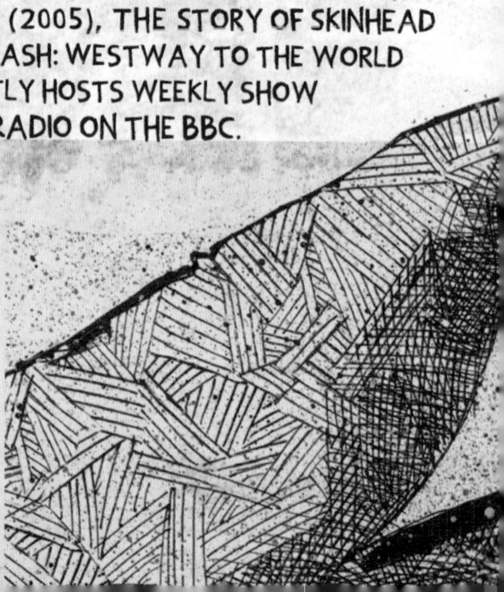

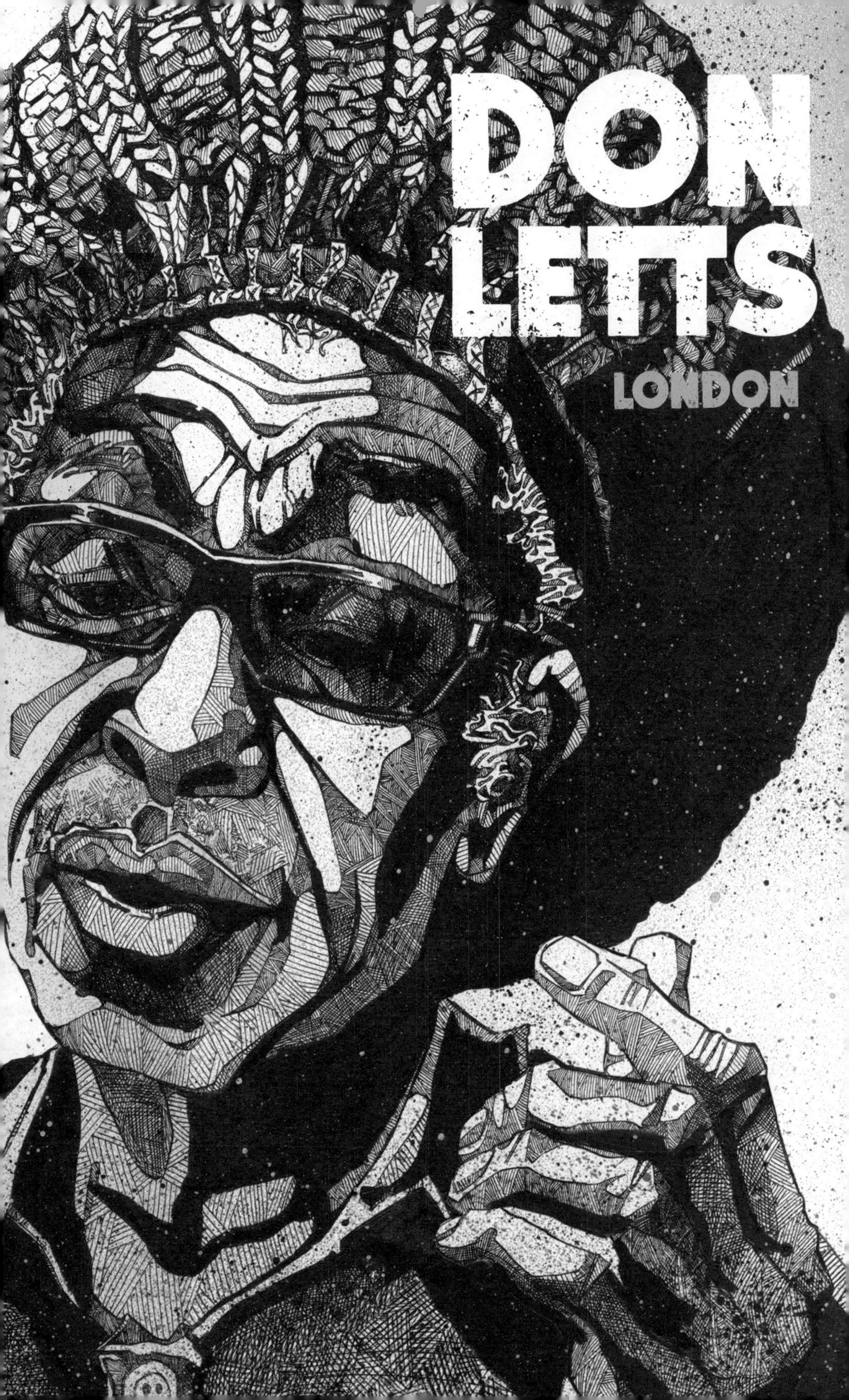
DON
LETTS
LONDON

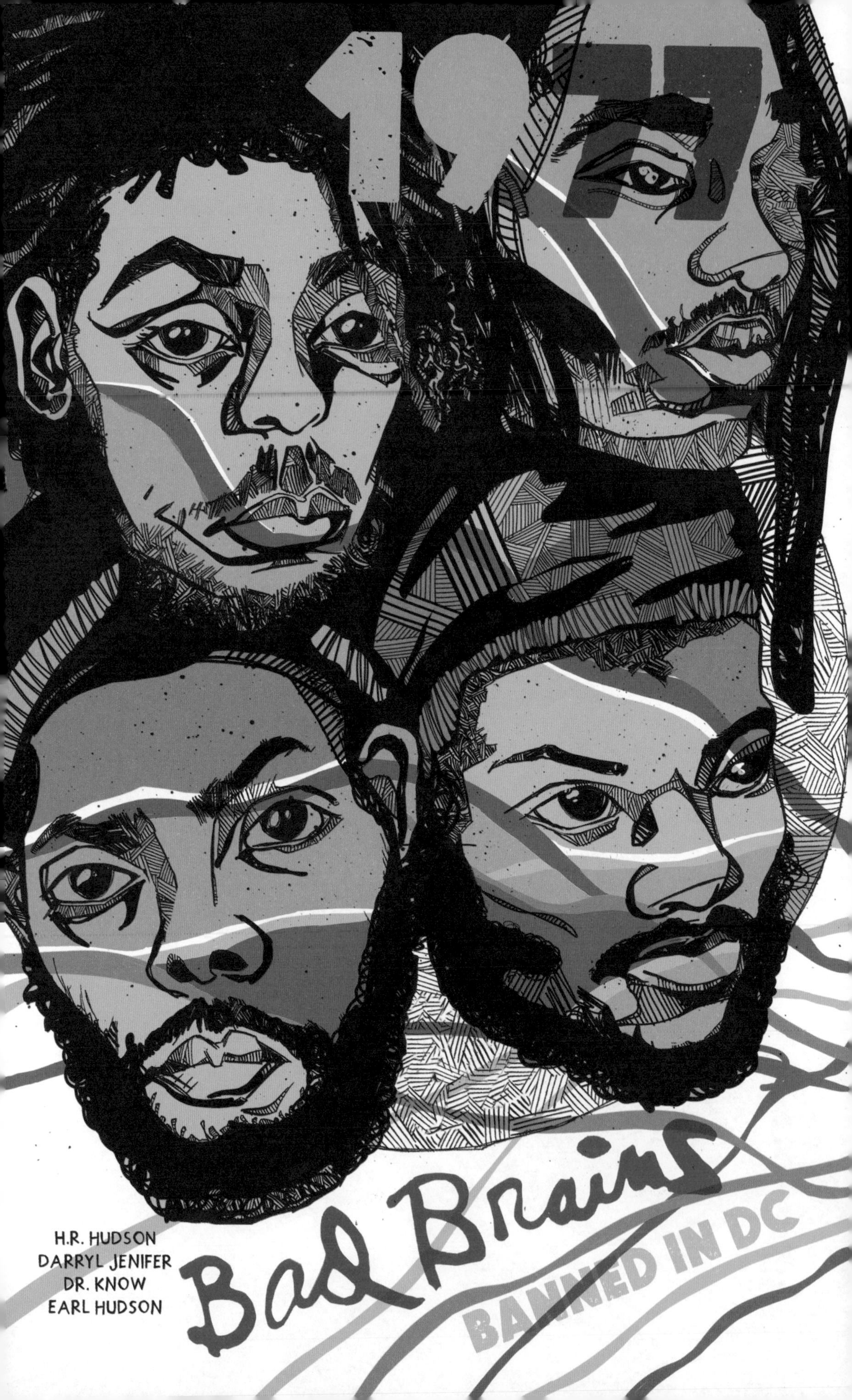
1977
H.R. HUDSON
DARRYL JENIFER
DR. KNOW
EARL HUDSON
Bad Brains
BANNED IN DC

HAVE YOU EVER HEARD OF BAD BRAINS I BET YOU
LOVE BAD BRAINS YOU REALLY NEED TO LISTEN TO
BAD BRAINS LET ME TELL YOU THE SIGNIFICANCE OF
BAD BRAINS YOU'RE BLACK AND YOU'VE NEVER
HEARD OF BAD BRAINS I BET BAD BRAINS IS YOUR
FAVORITE BAND OF COURSE YOU WOULD LIKE BAD
BRAINS BAD BRAINS HEY YOU LIKE BAD BRAINS

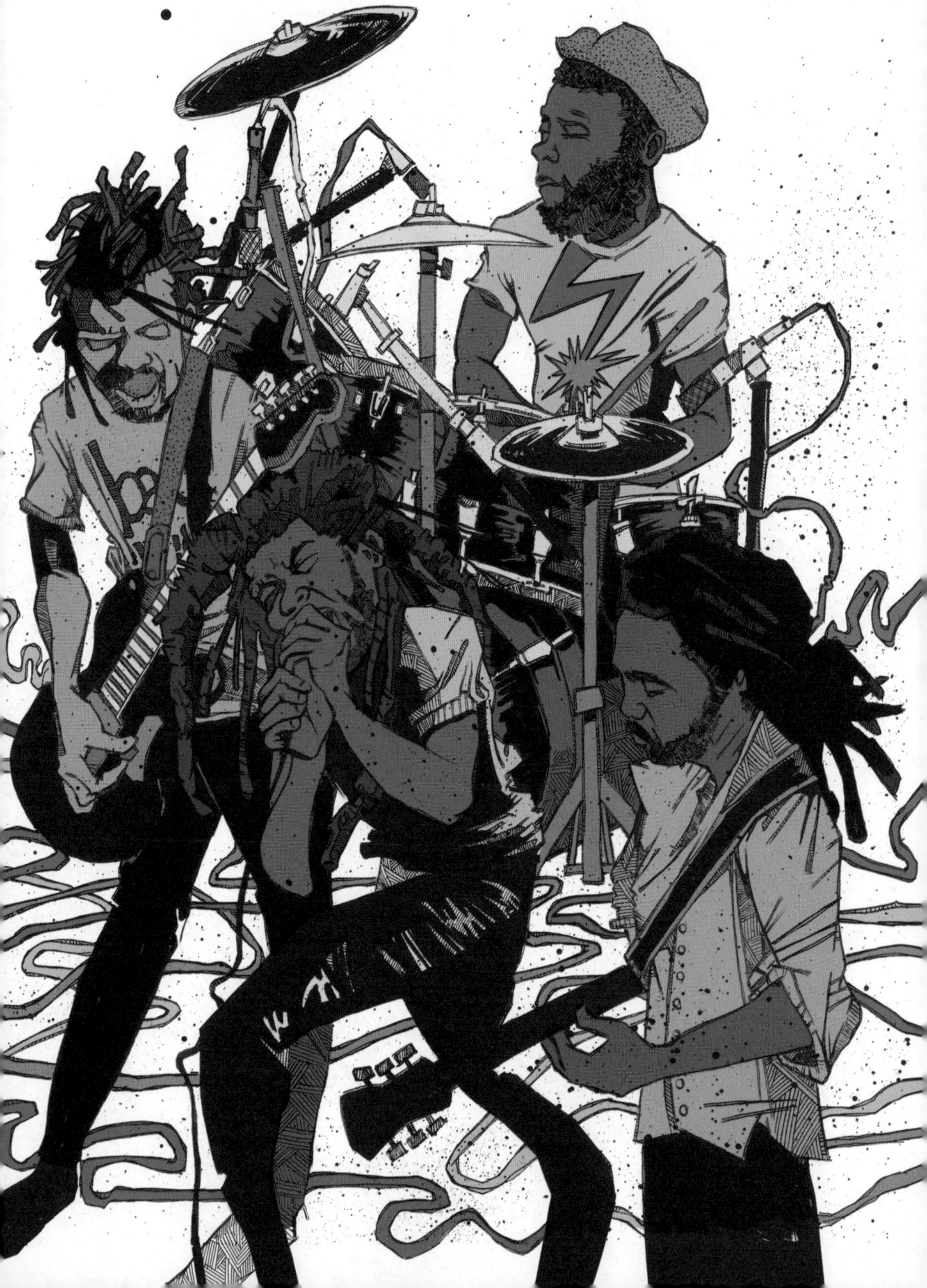

Black Death

CLASSIC LINEUP:

GREG HICKS: GUITAR
SIKI SPACEK: VOCALS, GUITAR
PHIL BULLARD: DRUMS
DARRELL HARRIS: BASS

CLEVELAND METAL BAND BREAK

LISTEN THIS ISN'T A PUNK BAND BUT SOMETIMES WHEN I SEE SPIKES AND CHAINS, I JUST GET DRAWING AND I ASK QUESTIONS LATER.

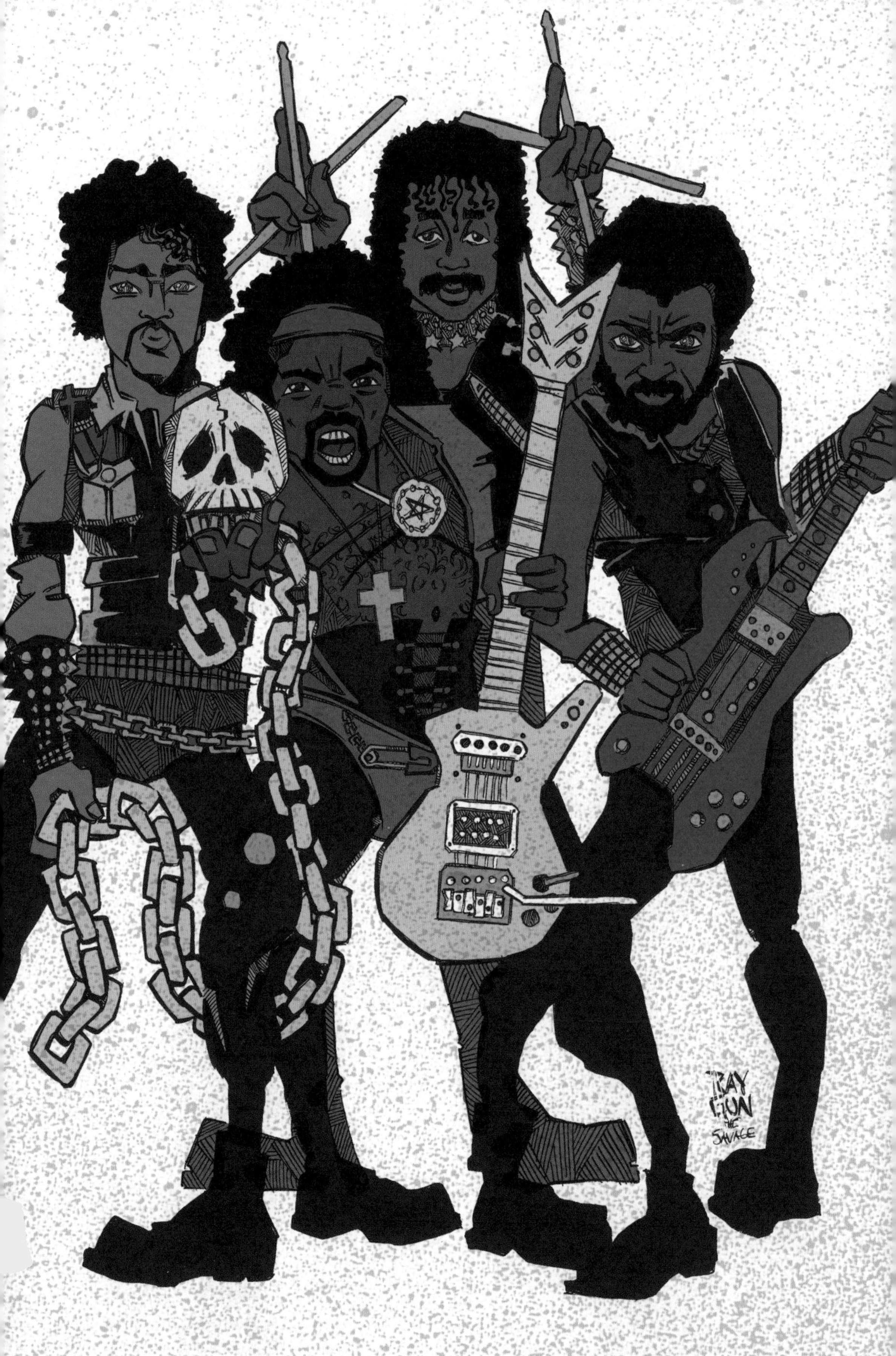
RAY GUN THE SAVAGE

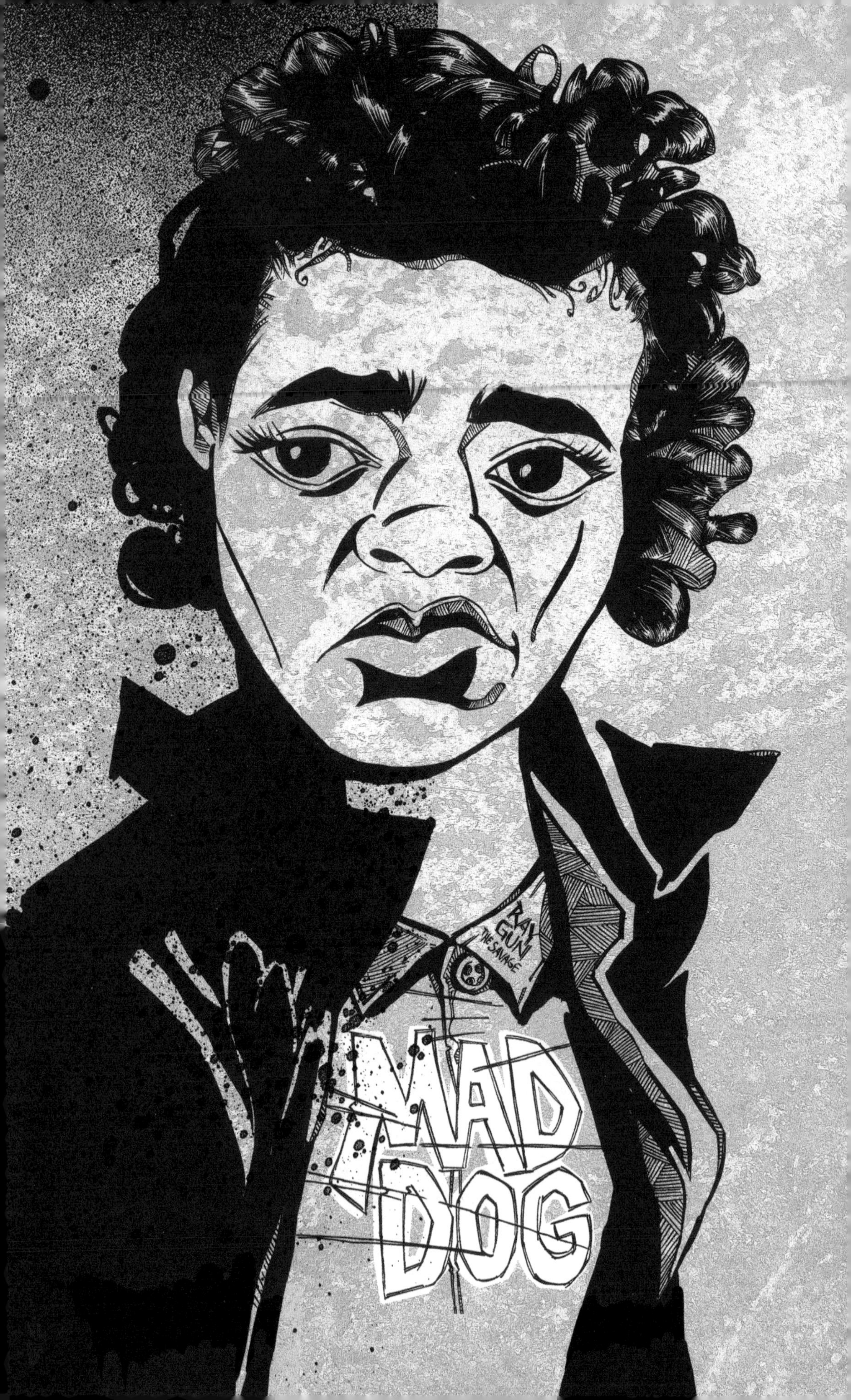
RAY GUN THE SAVAGE
MAD DOG

1978 L.A.

"I DON'T HAVE TIME FOR ANYBODY THAT'S LIKE PUNCHING THE CLOCK 9 TO 5, THAT'S THEIR WHOLE LIFE. DON'T YOU HAVE A PASSION? ISN'T THERE SOMETHING THAT YOU WOULD JUST DIE FOR, OR STARVE FOR? MUSIC IS IT FOR ME. YOU KNOW, IT'S A DISEASE AND THERE AIN'T NO CURE."

- MADDOG
Afro-Punk (the documentary)

KARLA MADDOG DUPLANTIER

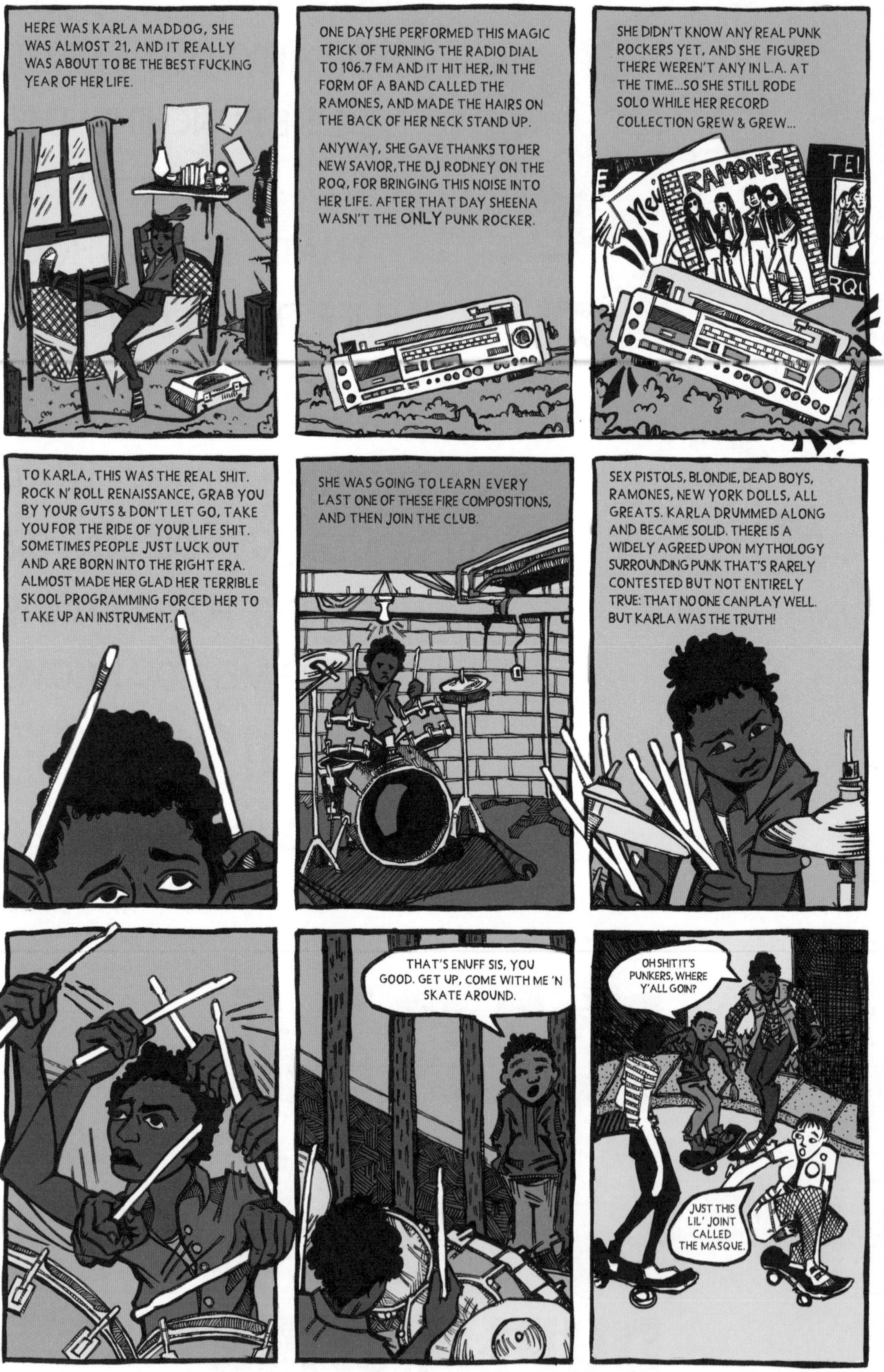
HERE WAS KARLA MADDOG, SHE WAS ALMOST 21, AND IT REALLY WAS ABOUT TO BE THE BEST FUCKING YEAR OF HER LIFE.
ONE DAY SHE PERFORMED THIS MAGIC TRICK OF TURNING THE RADIO DIAL TO 106.7 FM AND IT HIT HER, IN THE FORM OF A BAND CALLED THE RAMONES, AND MADE THE HAIRS ON THE BACK OF HER NECK STAND UP.
ANYWAY, SHE GAVE THANKS TO HER NEW SAVIOR, THE DJ RODNEY ON THE ROQ, FOR BRINGING THIS NOISE INTO HER LIFE. AFTER THAT DAY SHEENA WASN'T THE ONLY PUNK ROCKER.
SHE DIDN'T KNOW ANY REAL PUNK ROCKERS YET, AND SHE FIGURED THERE WEREN'T ANY IN L.A. AT THE TIME...SO SHE STILL RODE SOLO WHILE HER RECORD COLLECTION GREW & GREW...
RAMONES
TO KARLA, THIS WAS THE REAL SHIT. ROCK N' ROLL RENAISSANCE, GRAB YOU BY YOUR GUTS & DON'T LET GO, TAKE YOU FOR THE RIDE OF YOUR LIFE SHIT. SOMETIMES PEOPLE JUST LUCK OUT AND ARE BORN INTO THE RIGHT ERA. ALMOST MADE HER GLAD HER TERRIBLE SKOOL PROGRAMMING FORCED HER TO TAKE UP AN INSTRUMENT.
SHE WAS GOING TO LEARN EVERY LAST ONE OF THESE FIRE COMPOSITIONS, AND THEN JOIN THE CLUB.
SEX PISTOLS, BLONDIE, DEAD BOYS, RAMONES, NEW YORK DOLLS, ALL GREATS. KARLA DRUMMED ALONG AND BECAME SOLID. THERE IS A WIDELY AGREED UPON MYTHOLOGY SURROUNDING PUNK THAT'S RARELY CONTESTED BUT NOT ENTIRELY TRUE: THAT NO ONE CAN PLAY WELL. BUT KARLA WAS THE TRUTH!
THAT'S ENUFF SIS, YOU GOOD. GET UP, COME WITH ME 'N SKATE AROUND.
OH SHIT IT'S PUNKERS, WHERE Y'ALL GOIN?
JUST THIS LIL' JOINT CALLED THE MASQUE.

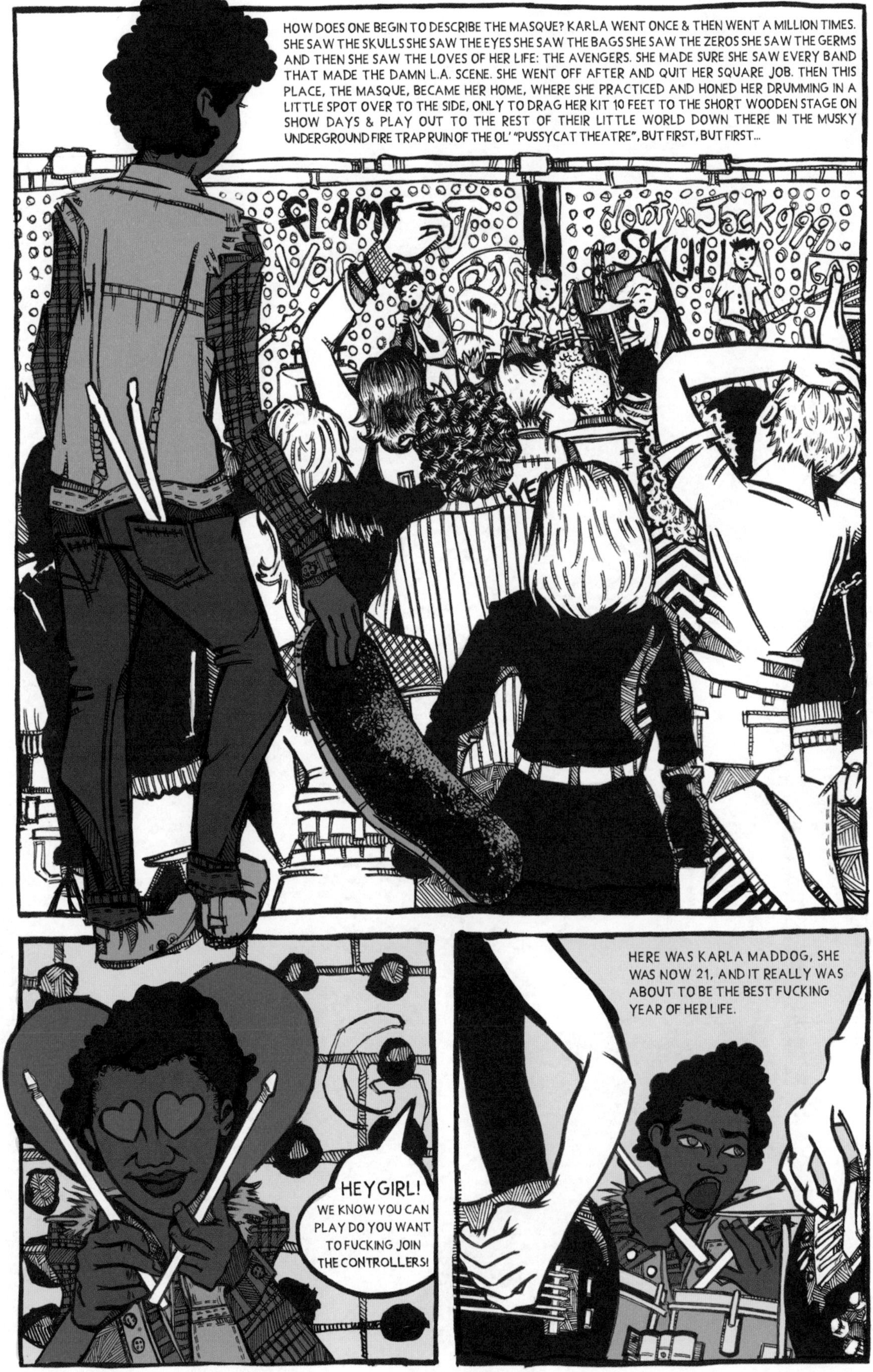
HOW DOES ONE BEGIN TO DESCRIBE THE MASQUE? KARLA WENT ONCE & THEN WENT A MILLION TIMES. SHE SAW THE SKULLS SHE SAW THE EYES SHE SAW THE BAGS SHE SAW THE ZEROS SHE SAW THE GERMS AND THEN SHE SAW THE LOVES OF HER LIFE: THE AVENGERS. SHE MADE SURE SHE SAW EVERY BAND THAT MADE THE DAMN L.A. SCENE. SHE WENT OFF AFTER AND QUIT HER SQUARE JOB. THEN THIS PLACE, THE MASQUE, BECAME HER HOME, WHERE SHE PRACTICED AND HONED HER DRUMMING IN A LITTLE SPOT OVER TO THE SIDE, ONLY TO DRAG HER KIT 10 FEET TO THE SHORT WOODEN STAGE ON SHOW DAYS & PLAY OUT TO THE REST OF THEIR LITTLE WORLD DOWN THERE IN THE MUSKY UNDERGROUND FIRE TRAP RUIN OF THE OL' "PUSSYCAT THEATRE", BUT FIRST, BUT FIRST...
HEY GIRL! WE KNOW YOU CAN PLAY DO YOU WANT TO FUCKING JOIN THE CONTROLLERS!
HERE WAS KARLA MADDOG, SHE WAS NOW 21, AND IT REALLY WAS ABOUT TO BE THE BEST FUCKING YEAR OF HER LIFE.

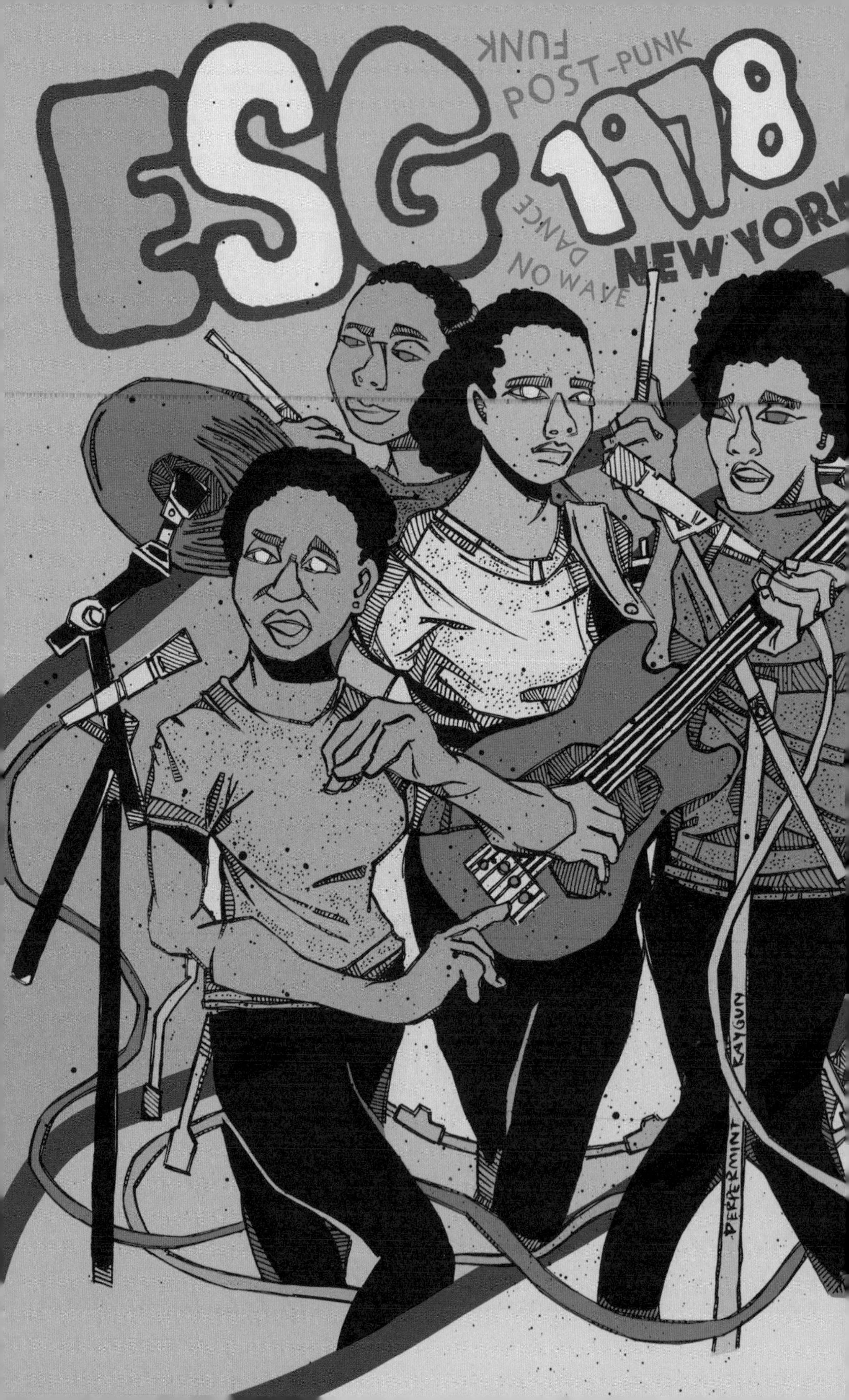
ESG
FUNK
POST-PUNK
1978
DANCE
NO WAVE
NEW YORK
KAYGUN
PEPPERMINT

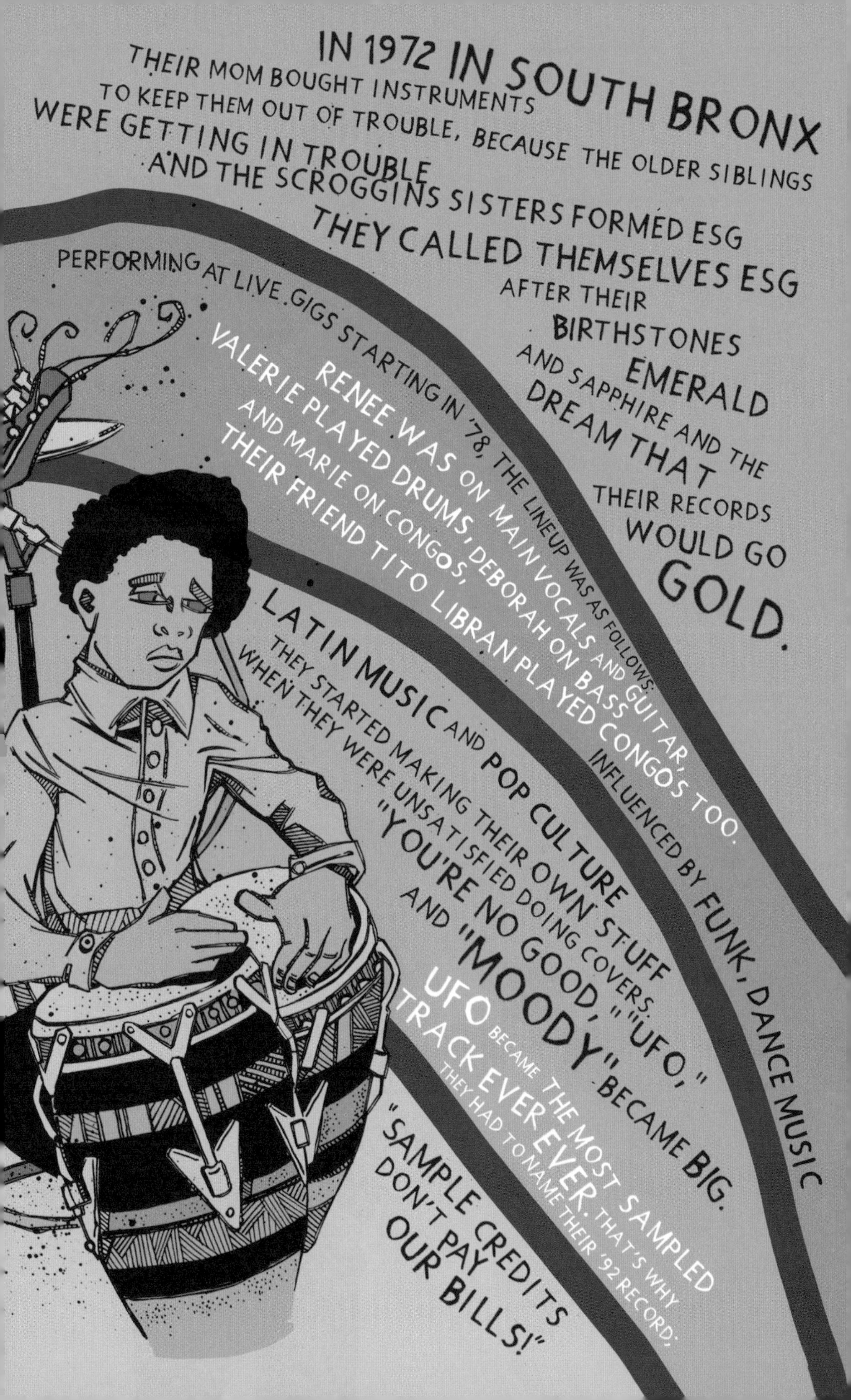
IN 1972 IN SOUTH BRONX
THEIR MOM BOUGHT INSTRUMENTS
TO KEEP THEM OUT OF TROUBLE, BECAUSE THE OLDER SIBLINGS
WERE GETTING IN TROUBLE
AND THE SCROGGINS SISTERS FORMED ESG
THEY CALLED THEMSELVES ESG
AFTER THEIR
BIRTHSTONES
EMERALD
AND SAPPHIRE AND THE
DREAM THAT
THEIR RECORDS
WOULD GO
GOLD.
PERFORMING AT LIVE GIGS STARTING IN '78, THE LINEUP WAS AS FOLLOWS:
RENEE WAS ON MAIN VOCALS AND GUITAR,
VALERIE PLAYED DRUMS, DEBORAH ON BASS
AND MARIE ON CONGOS,
THEIR FRIEND TITO LIBRAN PLAYED CONGOS TOO.
INFLUENCED BY FUNK, DANCE MUSIC
LATIN MUSIC AND POP CULTURE
THEY STARTED MAKING THEIR OWN STUFF
WHEN THEY WERE UNSATISFIED DOING COVERS.
"YOU'RE NO GOOD," "UFO,"
AND "MOODY" BECAME BIG.
UFO BECAME THE MOST SAMPLED
TRACK EVER EVER. THAT'S WHY
THEY HAD TO NAME THEIR '92 RECORD:
"SAMPLE CREDITS
DON'T PAY
OUR BILLS!"

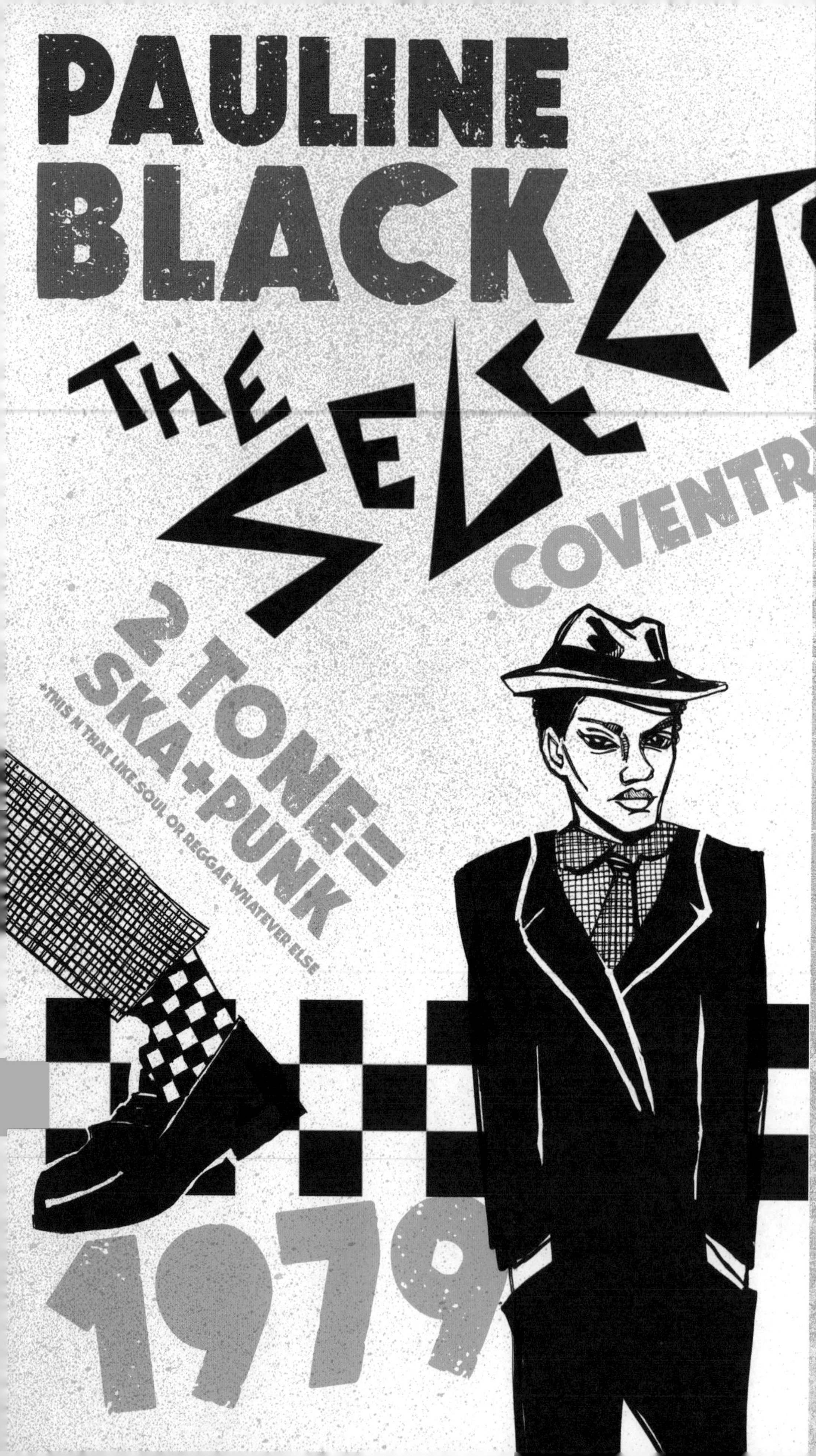
PAULINE
BLACK
THE SELECTE
COVENTRY
2 TONE = SKA + PUNK
+THIS N THAT LIKE SOUL OR REGGAE WHATEVER ELSE
1979

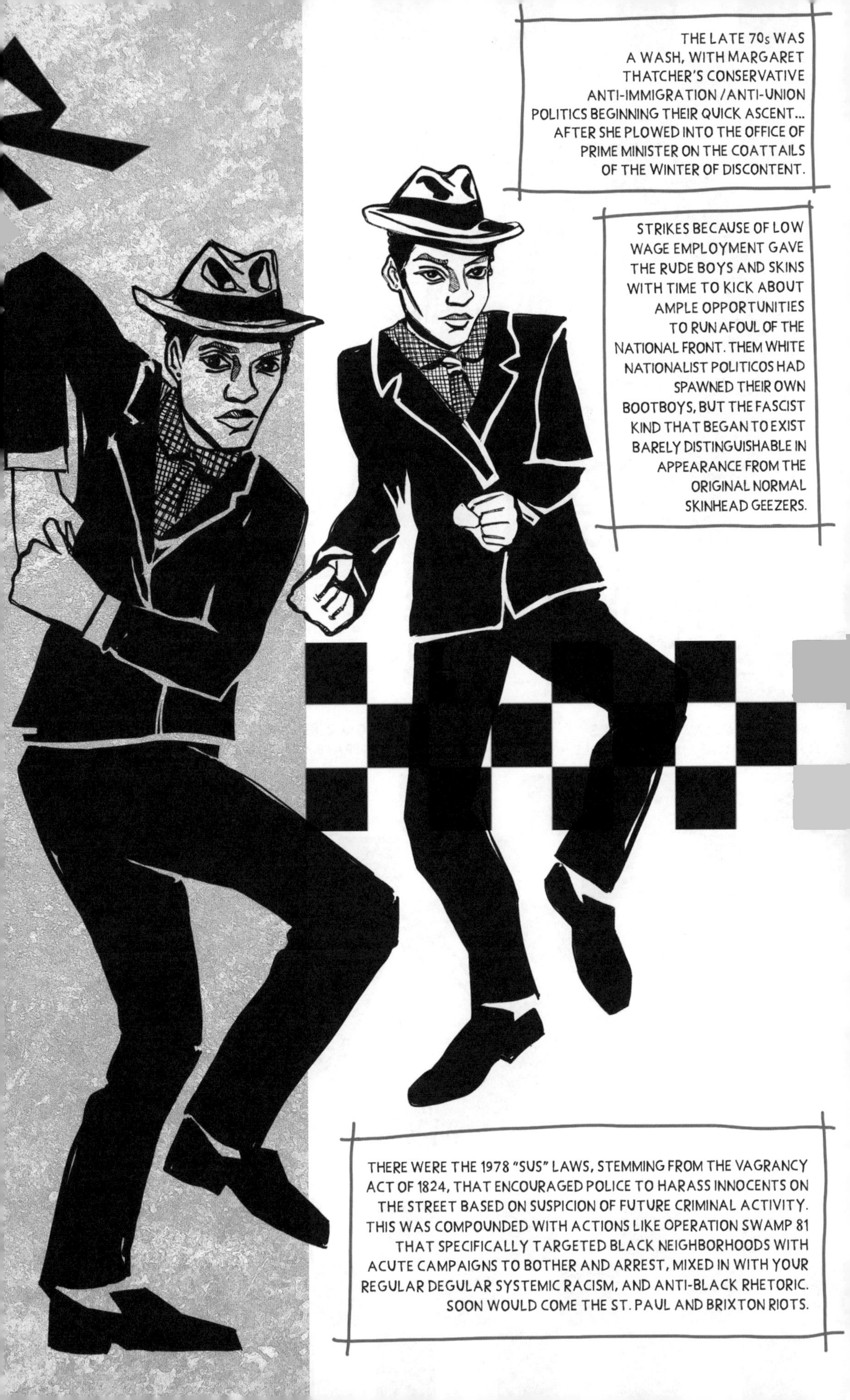
THE LATE 70s WAS A WASH, WITH MARGARET THATCHER'S CONSERVATIVE ANTI-IMMIGRATION / ANTI-UNION POLITICS BEGINNING THEIR QUICK ASCENT... AFTER SHE PLOWED INTO THE OFFICE OF PRIME MINISTER ON THE COATTAILS OF THE WINTER OF DISCONTENT.
STRIKES BECAUSE OF LOW WAGE EMPLOYMENT GAVE THE RUDE BOYS AND SKINS WITH TIME TO KICK ABOUT AMPLE OPPORTUNITIES TO RUN AFOUL OF THE NATIONAL FRONT. THEM WHITE NATIONALIST POLITICOS HAD SPAWNED THEIR OWN BOOTBOYS, BUT THE FASCIST KIND THAT BEGAN TO EXIST BARELY DISTINGUISHABLE IN APPEARANCE FROM THE ORIGINAL NORMAL SKINHEAD GEEZERS.
THERE WERE THE 1978 "SUS" LAWS, STEMMING FROM THE VAGRANCY ACT OF 1824, THAT ENCOURAGED POLICE TO HARASS INNOCENTS ON THE STREET BASED ON SUSPICION OF FUTURE CRIMINAL ACTIVITY. THIS WAS COMPOUNDED WITH ACTIONS LIKE OPERATION SWAMP 81 THAT SPECIFICALLY TARGETED BLACK NEIGHBORHOODS WITH ACUTE CAMPAIGNS TO BOTHER AND ARREST, MIXED IN WITH YOUR REGULAR DEGULAR SYSTEMIC RACISM, AND ANTI-BLACK RHETORIC. SOON WOULD COME THE ST. PAUL AND BRIXTON RIOTS.

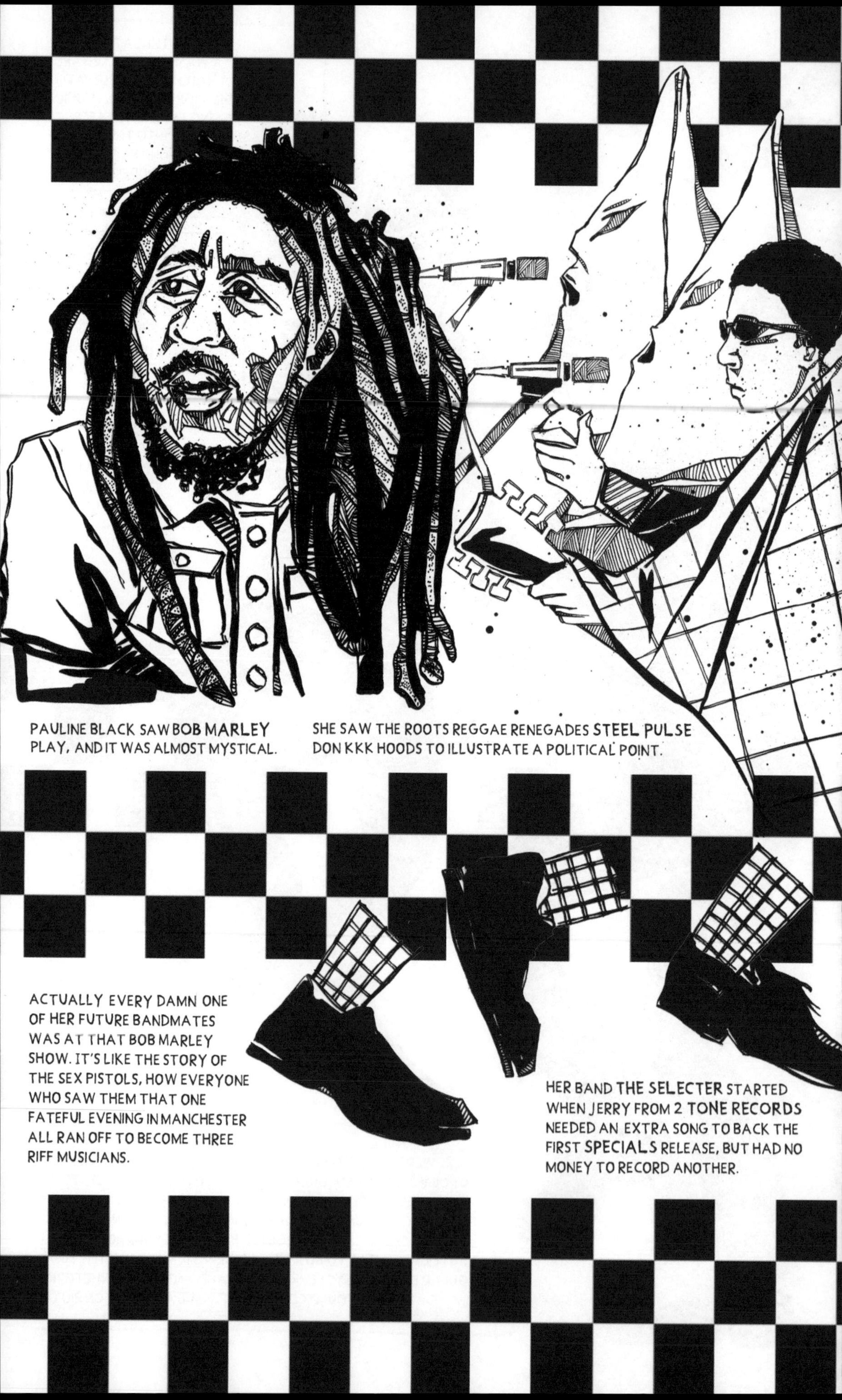
PAULINE BLACK SAW BOB MARLEY PLAY, AND IT WAS ALMOST MYSTICAL.
SHE SAW THE ROOTS REGGAE RENEGADES STEEL PULSE DON KKK HOODS TO ILLUSTRATE A POLITICAL POINT.
ACTUALLY EVERY DAMN ONE OF HER FUTURE BANDMATES WAS AT THAT BOB MARLEY SHOW. IT'S LIKE THE STORY OF THE SEX PISTOLS, HOW EVERYONE WHO SAW THEM THAT ONE FATEFUL EVENING IN MANCHESTER ALL RAN OFF TO BECOME THREE RIFF MUSICIANS.
HER BAND THE SELECTER STARTED WHEN JERRY FROM 2 TONE RECORDS NEEDED AN EXTRA SONG TO BACK THE FIRST SPECIALS RELEASE, BUT HAD NO MONEY TO RECORD ANOTHER.

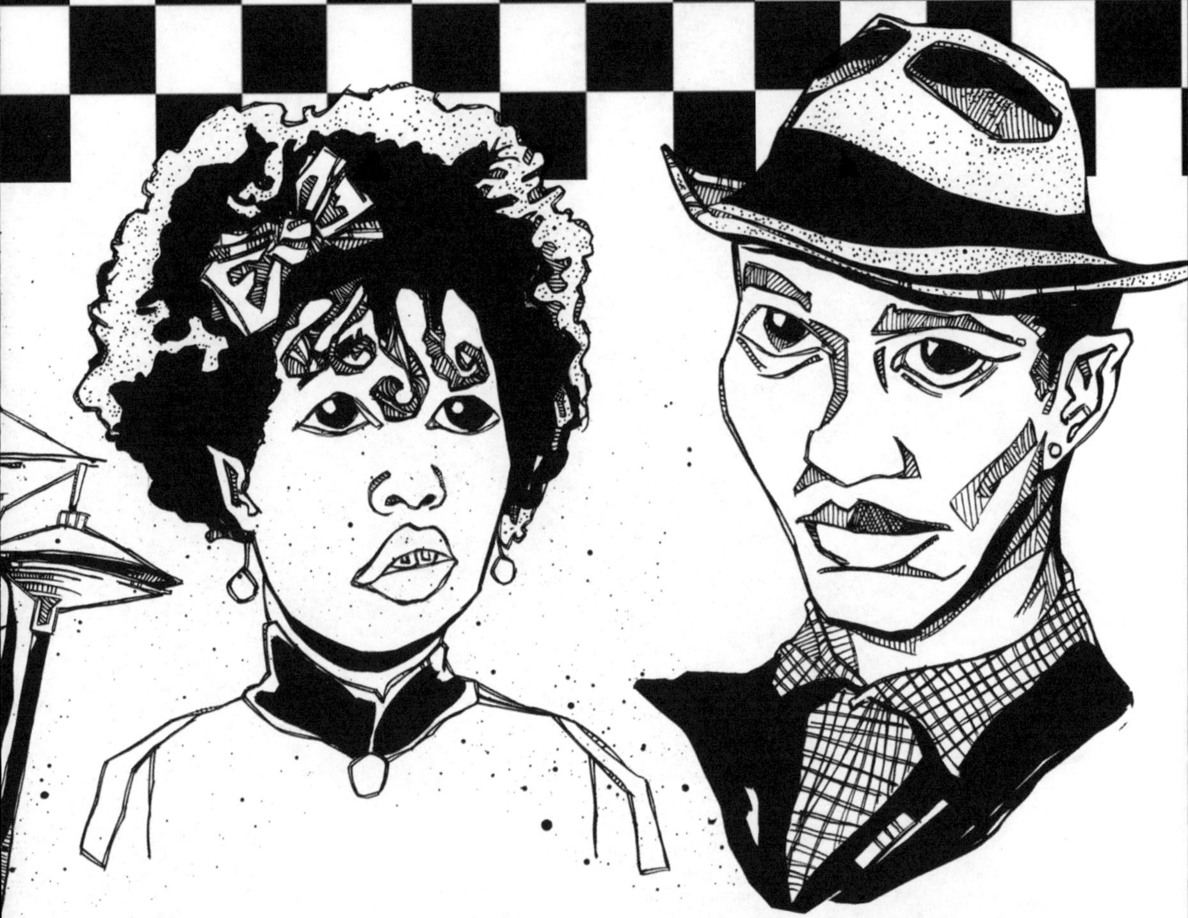

SHE SAW **POLY STYRENE** MAKING ANTI-COMMODITY ANTHEMS AND REFUSING TO DUMB HERSELF DOWN.

AND THEN, SHE WANTED TO TALK TO THE WORLD TOO. THE STREETS WERE TENSE, AND SHE WAS ANGRY.

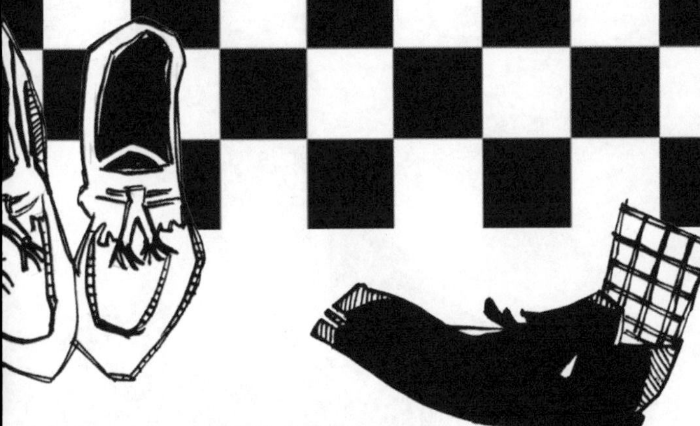

THEY TACKED ON **NEOL DAVIES'** SONG "THE SELECTER" AS THE B-SIDE, AND AFTER THAT DAVIES JUST KIND OF FORMED A BAND AROUND IT. PAULINE JOINED IN 1979.

2 TONE WAS A MULTI-RACIAL GENRE FULL OF PORK PIES AND WALT JABSCOs, AND GIGS THAT HAD INTRABAND WHITE AND BLACK MEMBERS WHO WANTED TO CREATE SOLIDARITY IN THE FACE OF THE RACIST POLITICAL CLIMATE. IT ONLY LASTED A FEW YEARS IN THE BEGINNING. BUT PAULINE IS BACK TOURING WITH HER RUDIES NOW AND TO BE HONEST, THE WORLD? PRETTY MUCH A REAL MESS. EVERYONE WOULD ALL STILL LIKE A WORD.

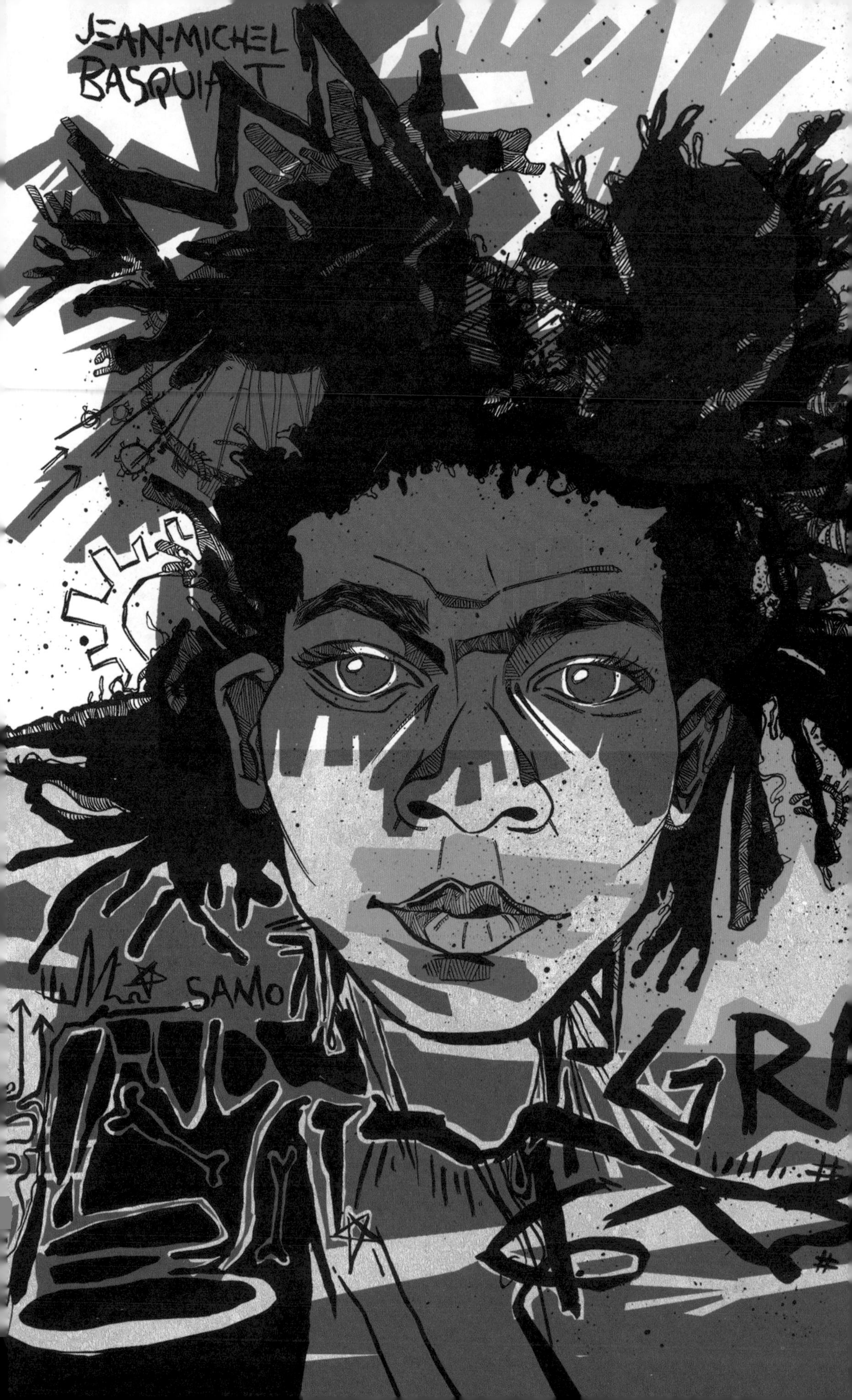
JEAN-MICHEL
BASQUIAT
SAMO

JEAN-MICHEL BASQUIAT MET MICHÆL
HOLMAN AT THE CANAL ZONE PART Y
IN A TIME WHEN
NEW YORK WAS GRIMY BLEA K AND COR-
RUPT, LITERALLY BURN ING.

BASQUIAT
WAS AN ARTIST
WHO TA GGED OSTENTATIOUS PHRASES
UNDER THE NAME SAMO c
FOR THE CULTURE
AND PA INTED POLI TICAL AND SOCI AL
COM MENTARY IN VIVID REDS YE LLOWS
BLUES AND BLACKS

BASQUIAT CARRIED ANAT OMICAL
STRUCTU RES IN HIS HEAD UNTIL HIS BAND
BEC AME TO BE CALLED "GRAY"

BAS QUIAT , CLARINET, STRUCK THE TRIANGLE
RAKED A FILE AGAINST TAU T
GUITAR STR INGS
M ANNED A MO TORIZED SHOPPING CART
SPOKE FREE ASSOCI ATION TO
THE SUICIDE HOTLINE
WHILE HOLMAN PL AYED THE DRUMS
WITH MASKING TA PE

THE DNA OF AN EX HILARAT I NG
TENSE THICK SOUNDSCAPE TO THE
NEW YORK RENAISSANCE OF NOISE

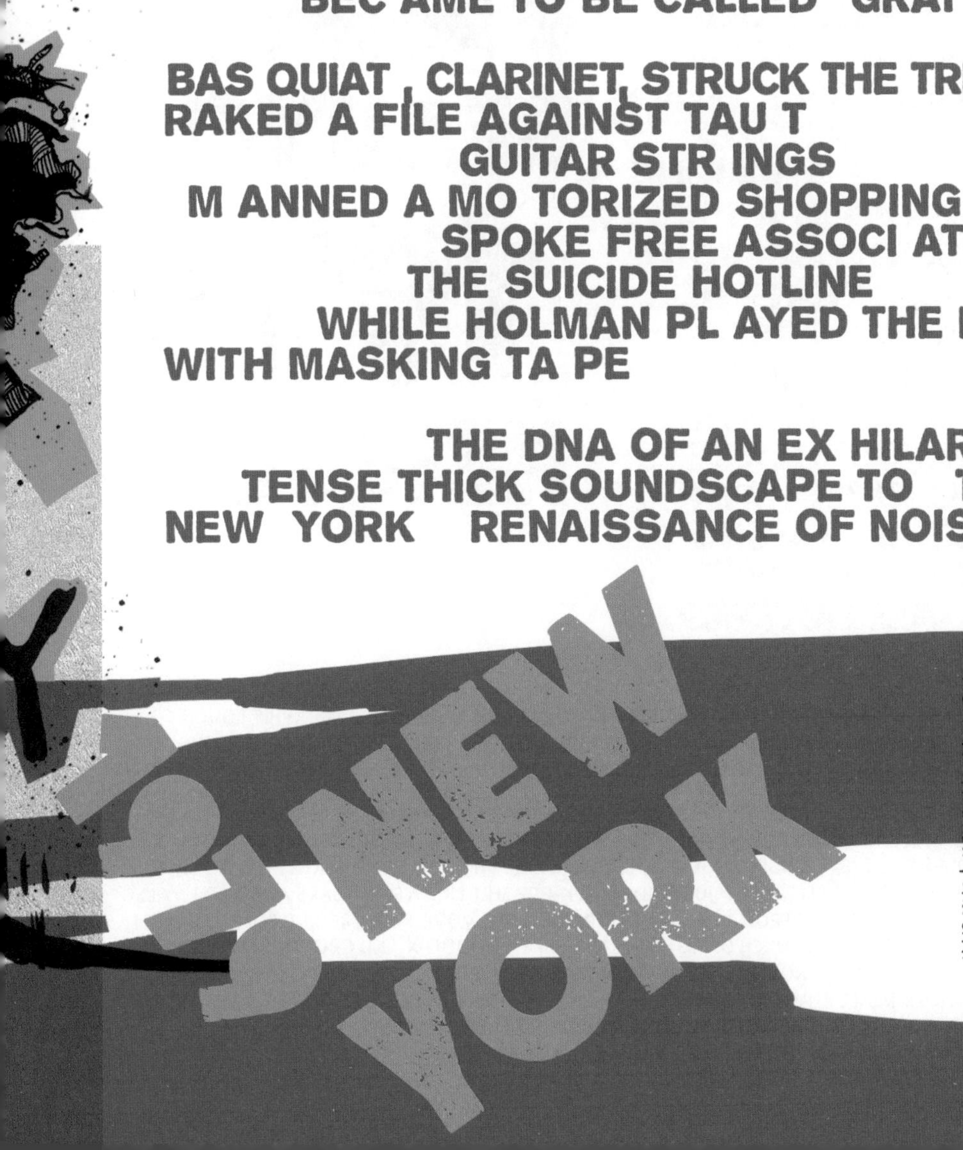
NEW
YORK

ALSO P.S. MICHAEL HOLMAN IS A TREASURE.
HE HELPED POPULARIZE THE ORIGINAL TERM "HIP-HOP"
AND WAS THE FIRST TO USE IT IN PRINT. HE IS THE MOST
ENTHUSIASTIC AND MESMERIZING STORYTELLER. HE
RESURRECTED GRAY IN 2010 TO PUT OUT THE RECORD
"SHADES OF GRAY" AND AGAIN RECENTLY WITH 2020s
"NEVER GONNA LEAVE NEW YORK CITY".

JEAN BEAUVOIR JOINED THE PUNK BAND PLASMATICS IN 1979 AND PLAYED BASS (AND SOMETIMES KEYS) ON **NEW HOPE FOR THE WRETCHED** AND **BEYOND THE VALLEY OF 1984.** THE CONTROVERSIAL METAL TINGED ACT WERE INSANELY SHOCKING FOR THEIR TIME, KNOWN FOR A STAGE SHOW THAT SABOTAGED CONSUMER PRODUCTS LIKE TVs AND CARS, BY SMASHING AND EXPLODING. SINGER WENDY O. WILLIAMS PLAYED A CHAINSAW AND GOT BEAT UP BY POLICE FOR THEIR SUPPOSED TRANSGRESSIONS, WHILE BEAUVOIR CO-WROTE BOPS LIKE THE STRAIGHT FORWARD "PIG IS A PIG." FOR CONCERTS HE WORE FRESH WHITE THREADS FROM HEAD TO TOE: A SUIT AND COATTAILS, WHITE GLOVES AND TIE, FUTURISTIC SUNGLASSES AND A BLOND MOHAWK FASHIONED BY TAKING A GUILLOTINE (WELL, PROBABLY CLIPPERS) TO THE OUTERMOST EDGES OF HIS NATURAL.

JEAN BEAUVOIR 1979 NEW YORK

HE PRODUCED RAMONES ALBUMS "ANIMAL BOY" (1986) AND "BRAIN DRAIN" (1989) LENDING HIS TOUCH TO HITS LIKE "PET SEMATARY," "MERRY CHRISTMAS (I DON'T WANT TO FIGHT TONIGHT)," AND CO-WRITING ANTI-REAGAN SONG "BONZO GOES TO BITBURG," PLAYING ADDITIONAL GUITAR, KEYS, AND BASS ON THE RECORDS.

BEAUVOIR STARTED HIS MUSICAL CAREER AT AGE 15 WITH HIS BAND TOPAZ, AND WENT ON TO PLAY MANY INSTRUMENTS, HOLD MANY INDUSTRY ROLES, AND WORK WITH SO MANY WELL REGARDED MUSICIANS LIKE WAY MORE THAN COULD FILL EVERY SINGLE PAGE OF THIS COMIC XINE THING SO TO BE HONEST I JUST PICKED OUT SOME OF THE PUNK STUFF. HE LITERALLY JUST DID SOME K-POP SHIT LIKE A FEW YEARS AGO AND HE ALSO MADE THAT "FEEL THE HEAT" JOINT FROM THE SYLVESTER STALLONE MOVIE FROM '86 AND SORRY I GUESS I SHOULD ADD THAT HE'S DEF DONE A BUNCH OF HIS OWN STUFF LIKE VOODOO X AND CROWN OF THORNS BUT OK I REALLY DO HAVE TO STOP NOW PLEASE DON'T BE MAD AT ME FOR NOT FOCUSING ON HIS SOLO PROJECTS, PLASMATICS IS REALLY JUST MY SHIT. GO WATCH LIVE VIDEOS OF THEM PLAYING TOGETHER AND WONDER HOW IN THE WORLD? ARE THEY NOT? MELTING PICKS? FIND THE NEW YORK PIER 62 VIDEO. ALSO, I JUST SAW THAT BEAUVOIR RELEASED A BIOGRAPHY IN MARCH 2022: "BET MY SOUL ON ROCK 'N' ROLL: DIARY OF A BLACK PUNK ICON," SO CHECK THAT OUT FOR SURE.

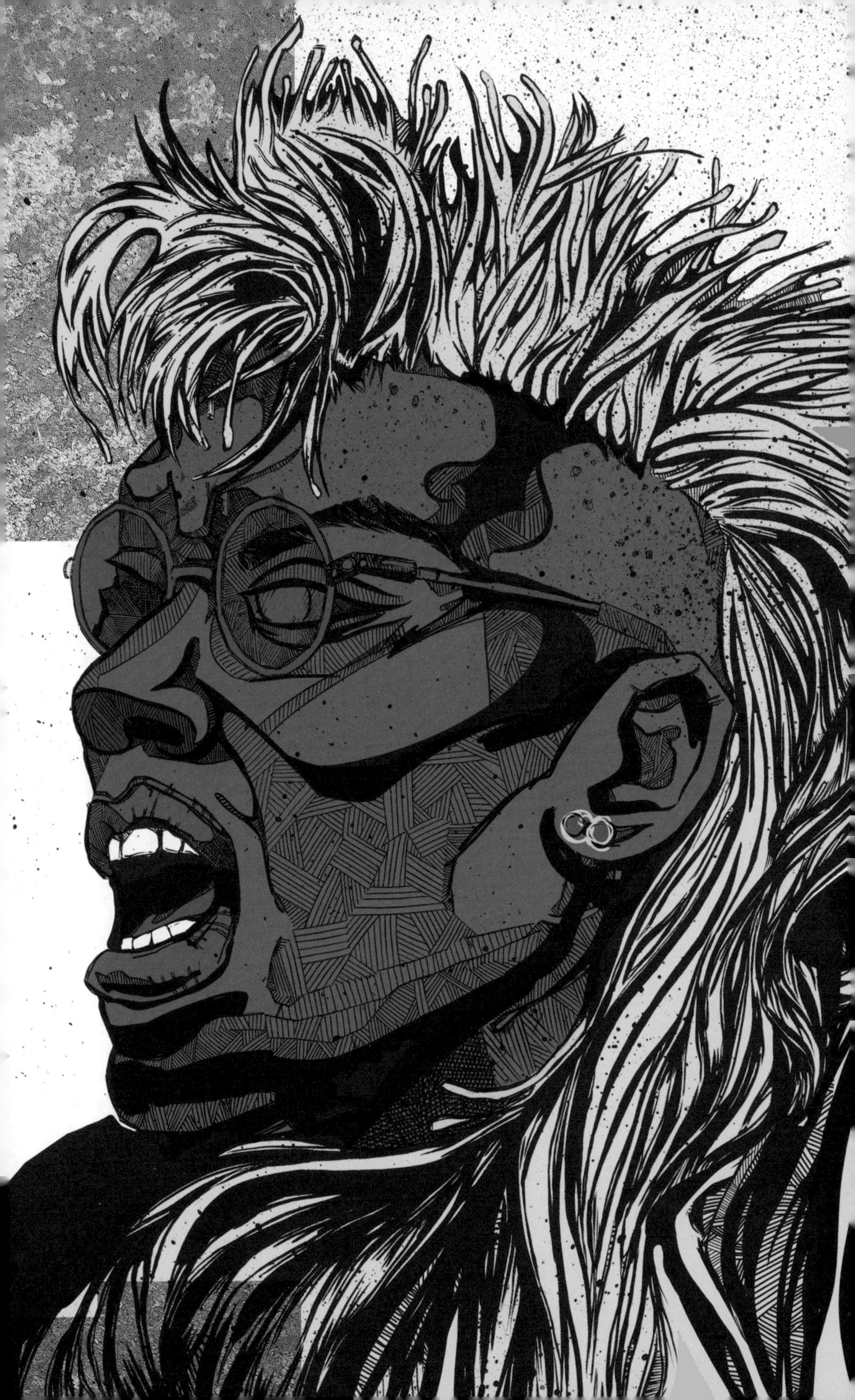

UP THE BLACK PUNKS

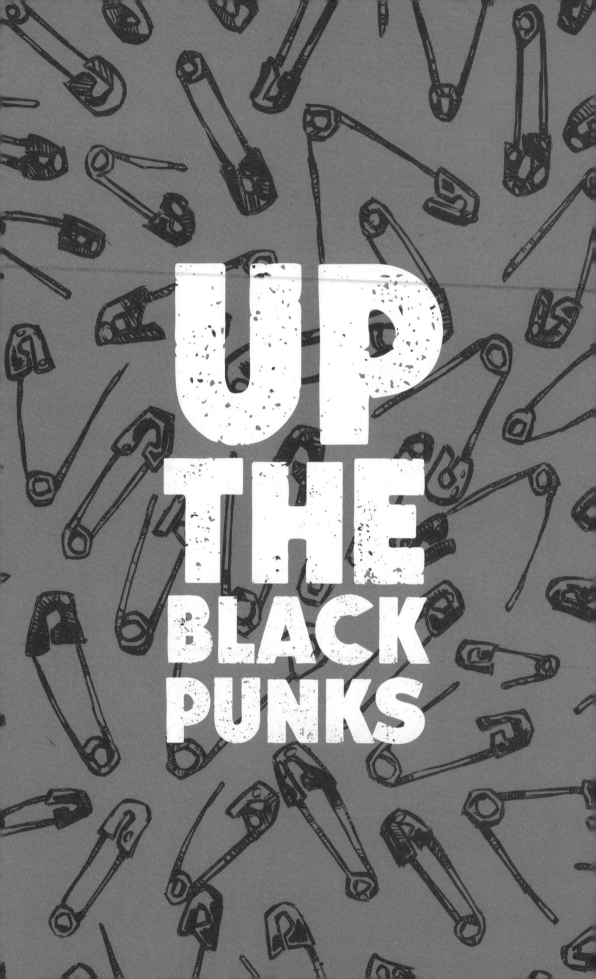

WARNING

OF THIS THING

THE LAST THIRD

IS MILDLY DISORDERED

CHRONOLOGICALLY

ON PUNK STUFF WITH HANIF ABDURRAQIB

WHILST CORRESPONDING WITH THE AUTHOR ABDURRAQIB, I, AN ADULT WITH FREEDOM TO ASK ANYTHING AT ALL, CHOSE TO ASK GATEKEEPING QUESTIONS ABOUT A MUSICAL GENRE THAT MOST TEENAGERS GROW OUT OF IN TWO YEARS TOPS.

INTERVIEW IS FROM 2019... PROVING THAT SOMETIMES THE ZINE **WILL** IN FACT **EVENTUALLY** COME OUT.

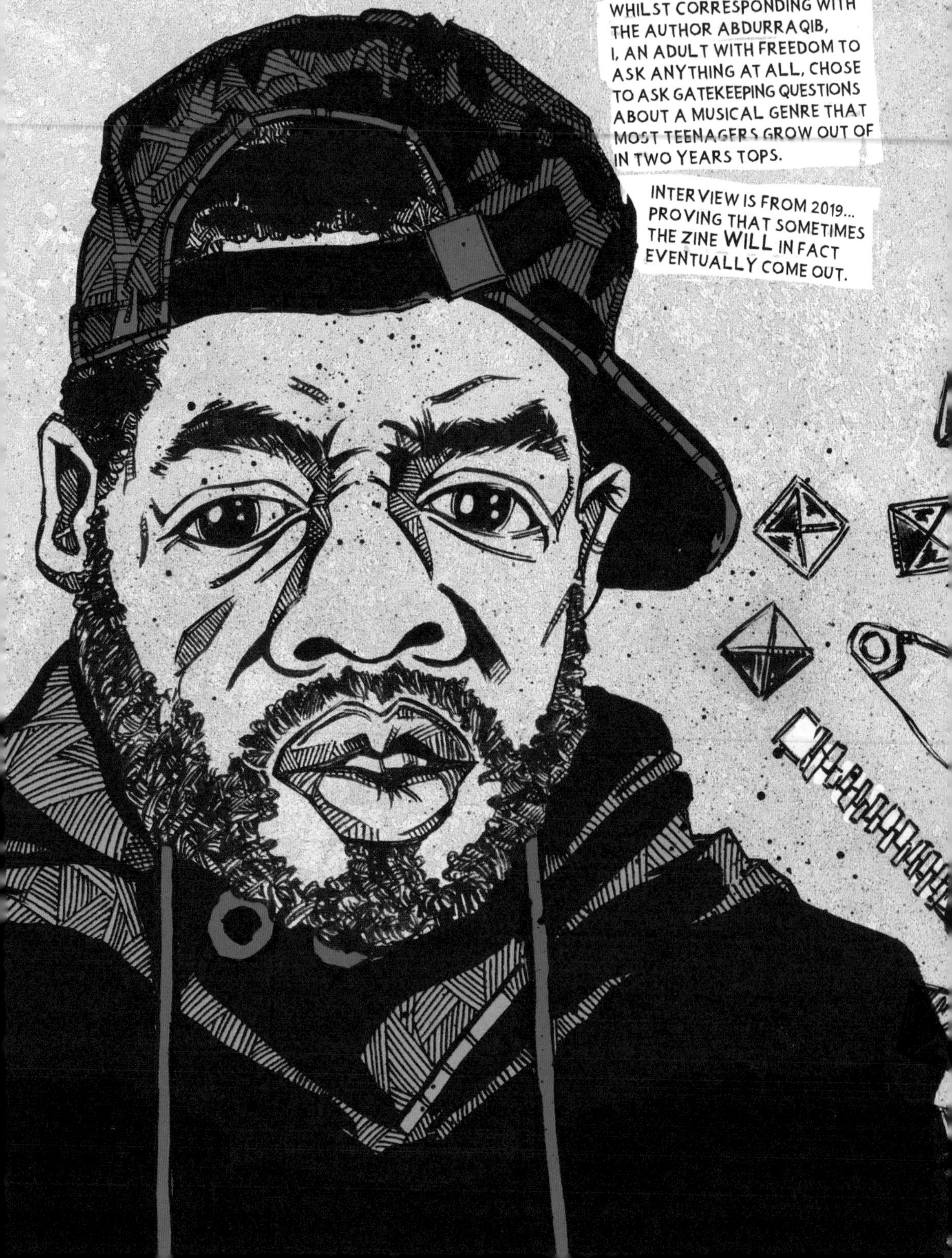

WHAT IS PUNK? WHAT DEFINES IT, WHAT DOES THAT WORD EVOKE IN YOU?

I THINK THERE ARE AS MANY WAYS TO DEFINE PUNK AS THERE ARE PEOPLE WHO HAVE IMMERSED THEMSELVES IN IT, OR PEOPLE WHO HAVE, FOR A MOMENT, FOUND THEMSELVES LOOKING FOR COMMUNITY AMONG A SEA OF PEOPLE WHO, PERHAPS, DID NOT LOOK LIKE THEM. AND SO I IMAGINE PUNK AS AN INTERNAL ENGINE FIRST. THE THING THAT BLOOMS OUT OF BEING ON THE OUTSKIRTS OF THE OUTSKIRTS. EVERYONE IMAGINES THEMSELVES AS HARDER TO UNDERSTAND THAN THEY ACTUALLY ARE, AND I ALWAYS FELT LIKE PUNK WAS A WAY FOR ME TO PERFORM THAT IN A WAY THAT WASN'T AS ABSURD AS I FELT ON THE INSIDE.

COULD YOU CRITIQUE AN ASPECT OF PUNK?

MAINSTREAM PUNK SPACES ARE STILL TOO WHITE, TOO MALE, TOO CIS, AND ARE SEEMINGLY UNWILLING TO IMAGINE THEMSELVES OUT OF THAT WAY OF THINKING.

DID PUNK END? WHAT IS ITS LEGACY?

I DON'T THINK IT DIED, BUT JUST LIKE ALL GENRES THAT INTERSECT WITH AN AESTHETIC, IT HAS BEEN COMMODIFIED, WHICH I THINK HAS MADE IT HARDER TO TRACE ITS ROOTS, RIGHT? WHENEVER AMERICA'S CAPITALISTIC AND COMMERCIAL INSTINCTS GET A HOLD OF ANY MOVEMENT, IT BLURS THE LINE BETWEEN THE ACCESSIBLE POPULARITY, AND THE VERY REAL HISTORY THAT DESIRES APPRECIATION. AND SO, ULTIMATELY, PUNK'S LEGACY IS THE LEGACY OF MOST MOVEMENTS THAT WERE CREATED BY THE MARGINALIZED AND SEEN AS PROFITABLE BY THE NON-MARGINALIZED. THE HEARTBEAT OF IT, IN MANY WAYS, IS KEPT ALIVE BY THOSE PEOPLE WHO ARE LESS AT THE FOREFRONT OF THE CONVERSATION.

TELL A SHORT STORY ABOUT SOMETHING YOU'VE SEEN OR DONE THAT PRETTY MUCH SUMS UP PUNK FOR YOU. I HAVE SURVIVED MANY THINGS THAT HAVE ATTEMPTED TO KILL ME, INCLUDING MYSELF.

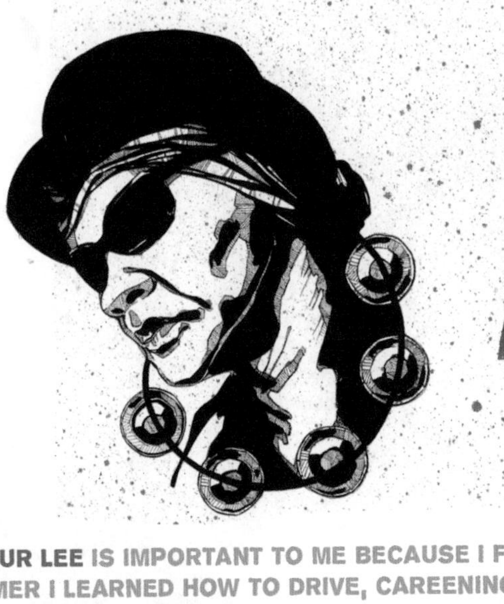

HANIF ON ARTHUR LEE OF LOVE

ARTHUR LEE IS IMPORTANT TO ME BECAUSE I FIRST HEARD **FOREVER CHANGES** IN THE SUMMER I LEARNED HOW TO DRIVE, CAREENING AROUND I-270 AND THINKING IT WAS THE MOST PERFECT RECORD I'D EVER HEARD. CRAFTED, I THOUGHT, PARTICULARLY FOR A NIGHT IN A CAR WITH BUSTED A/C, AND THE WINDOWS DOWN, AND THE MOON SEEMINGLY CLOSE ENOUGH TO BE A PASSENGER.

THE INFAMOUS JIMI/ARTHUR LEE JAM SESSION IS AS PUNK AS IT GETS, IF PEOPLE CAN FIND IT. I'M OFTEN SO HEARTBROKEN BY HIS LATER LIFE. HOW HE SO DESPERATELY WANTED TO REUNITE LOVE, BUT THEN WENT TO PRISON FOR NINE YEARS, AND THE OTHER MEMBERS DIED WHILE HE WAS LOCKED UP. HOW HE DIED WITH NO MONEY, FRIENDS HAVING TO RAISE CASH FOR HIS CANCER TREATMENTS. IT'S EASY TO ROMANTICIZE IT ALL, BUT THERE'S NOTHING ROMANTIC ABOUT DYING BROKE AND ALONE. NOT FOR ANYONE, BUT PARTICULARLY NOT FOR SOMEONE WHO GAVE SO MUCH.

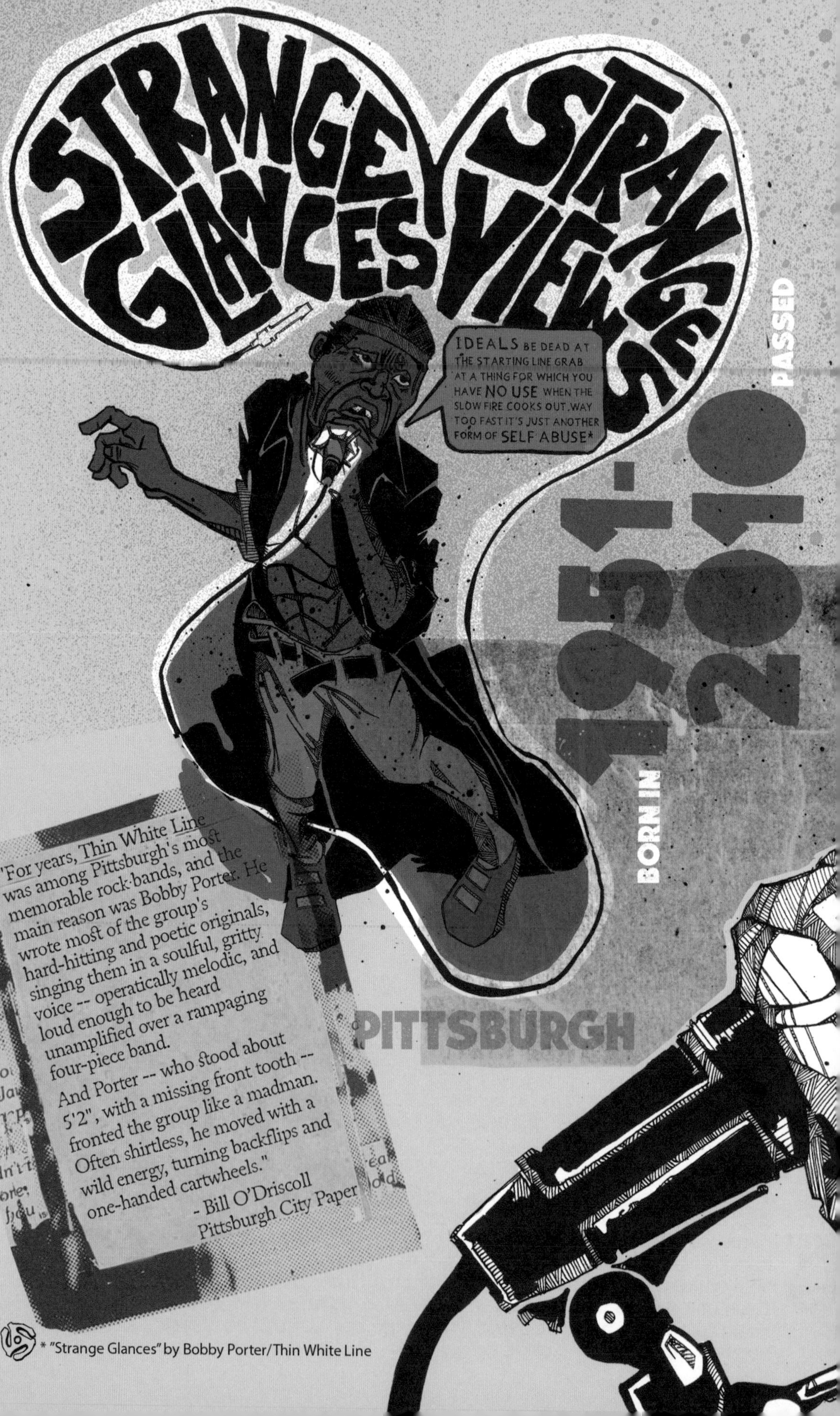

STRANGE GLANCES
STRANGE VIEWS
IDEALS BE DEAD AT THE STARTING LINE GRAB AT A THING FOR WHICH YOU HAVE NO USE WHEN THE SLOW FIRE COOKS OUT, WAY TOO FAST IT'S JUST ANOTHER FORM OF SELF ABUSE*
BORN IN
1951-
PITTSBURGH
PASSED
2010

"For years, Thin White Line was among Pittsburgh's most memorable rock bands, and the main reason was Bobby Porter. He wrote most of the group's hard-hitting and poetic originals, singing them in a soulful, gritty voice -- operatically melodic, and loud enough to be heard unamplified over a rampaging four-piece band.

And Porter -- who stood about 5'2", with a missing front tooth -- fronted the group like a madman. Often shirtless, he moved with a wild energy, turning backflips and one-handed cartwheels."

- Bill O'Driscoll
Pittsburgh City Paper

* "Strange Glances" by Bobby Porter/Thin White Line

BOBBY CLEO PORTER

BOBBY, THE PUNK ROCK OTIS REDDING, FRONTED OTIS AND THE RED Z, YOUNG LUST, THIN WHITE LINE, AND SHORT DARK STRANGERS. IN PERFORMANCE, HE COULD COMMAND A CHATTERING ROOM TO ATTENTION WITH THE POWER OF HIS IMPOSSIBLY EXCITING DELIVERY, OFTEN FROM THE FIRST LINES OF HIS OPENING ACAPELLA ARTICULATIONS.

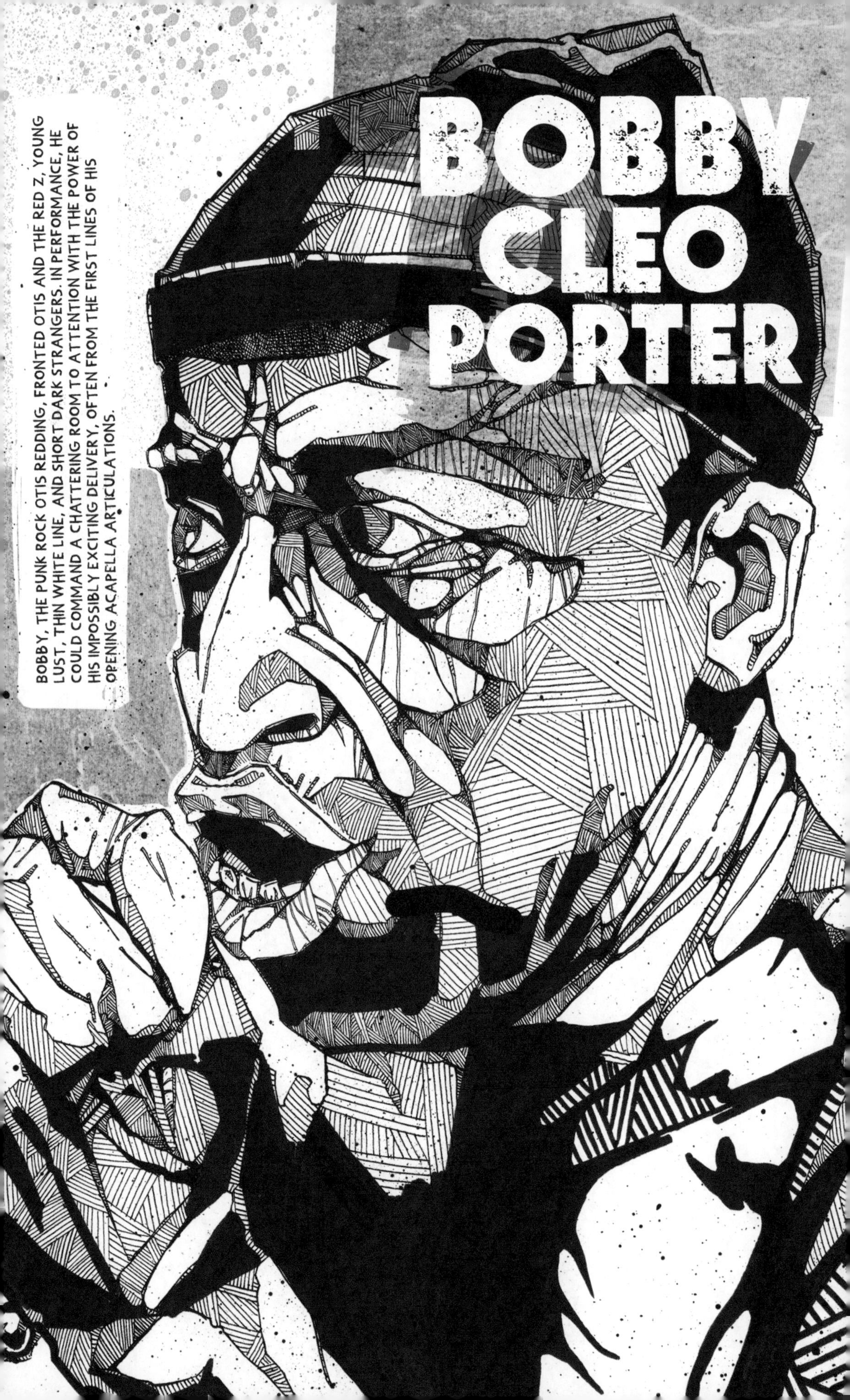

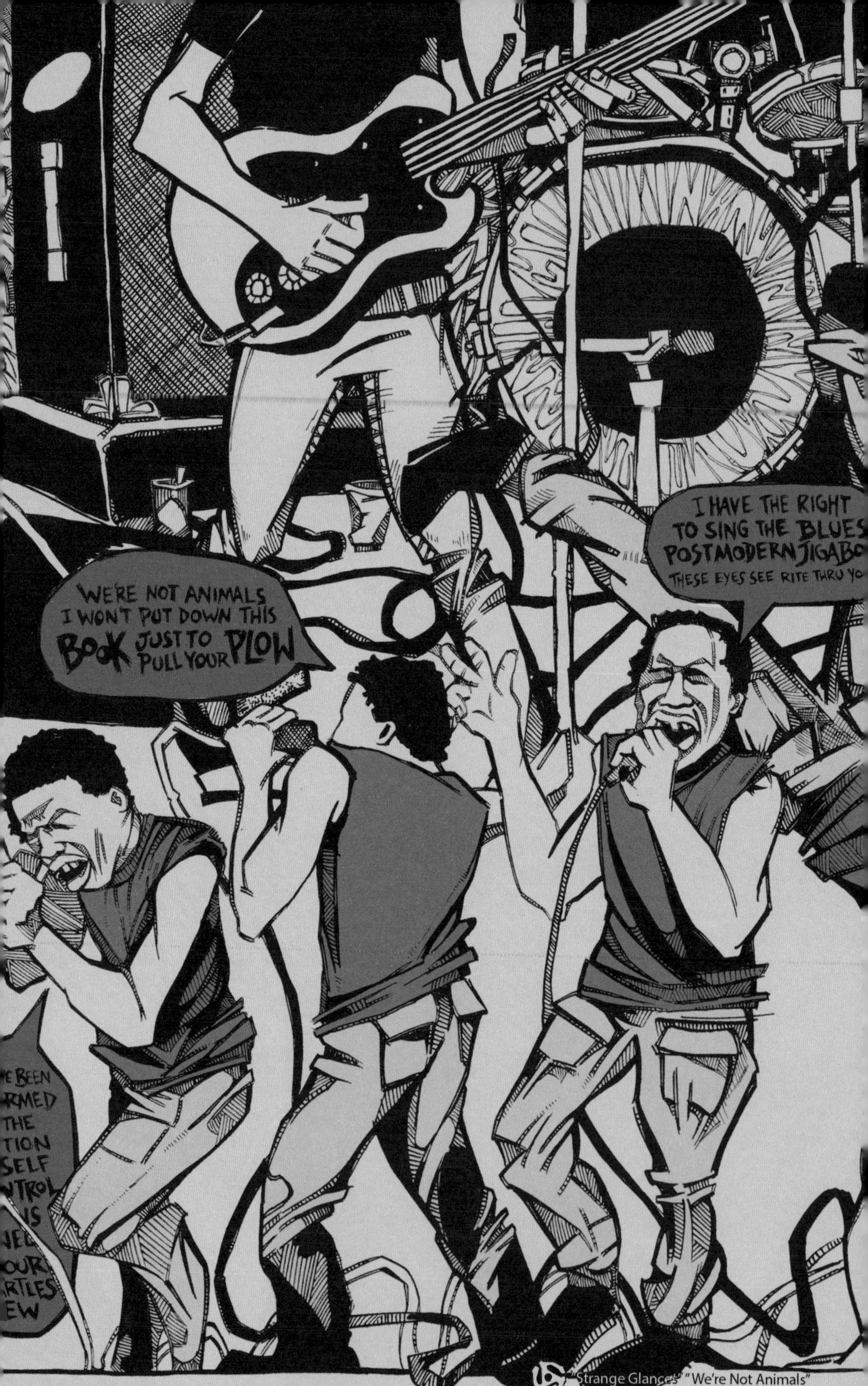
WE'RE NOT ANIMALS I WON'T PUT DOWN THIS BOOK JUST TO PULL YOUR PLOW
I HAVE THE RIGHT TO SING THE BLUES POSTMODERN JIGABO
THESE EYES SEE RITE THRU YO
E BEEN RMED THE TION SELF NTROL S JEL OUR RTLES EW

"Strange Glances" "We're Not Animals"

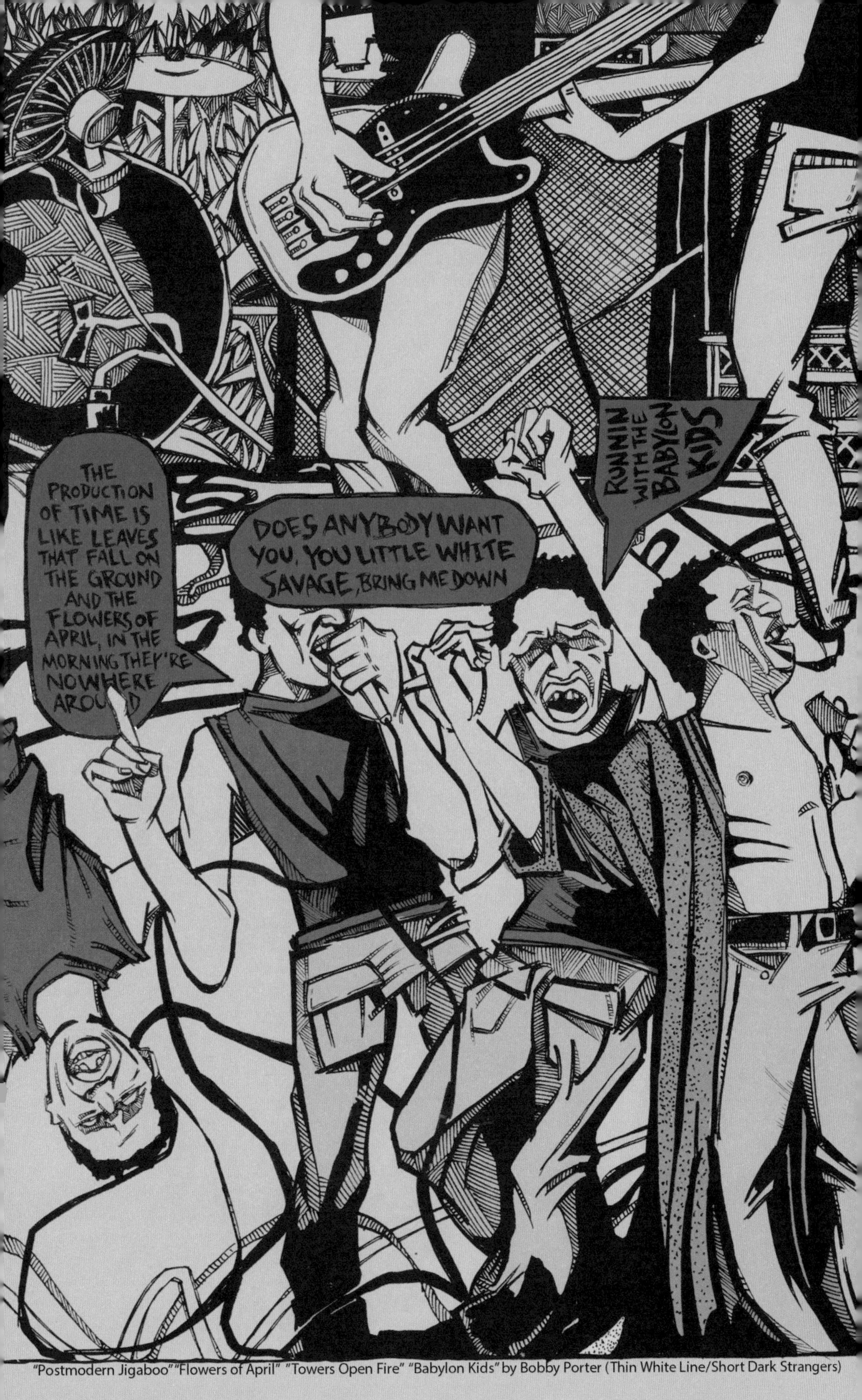
THE PRODUCTION OF TIME IS LIKE LEAVES THAT FALL ON THE GROUND AND THE FLOWERS OF APRIL, IN THE MORNING THEY'RE NOWHERE AROUND
DOES ANYBODY WANT YOU, YOU LITTLE WHITE SAVAGE, BRING ME DOWN
RUNNIN WITH THE BABYLON KIDS

"Postmodern Jigaboo" "Flowers of April" "Towers Open Fire" "Babylon Kids" by Bobby Porter (Thin White Line/Short Dark Strangers)

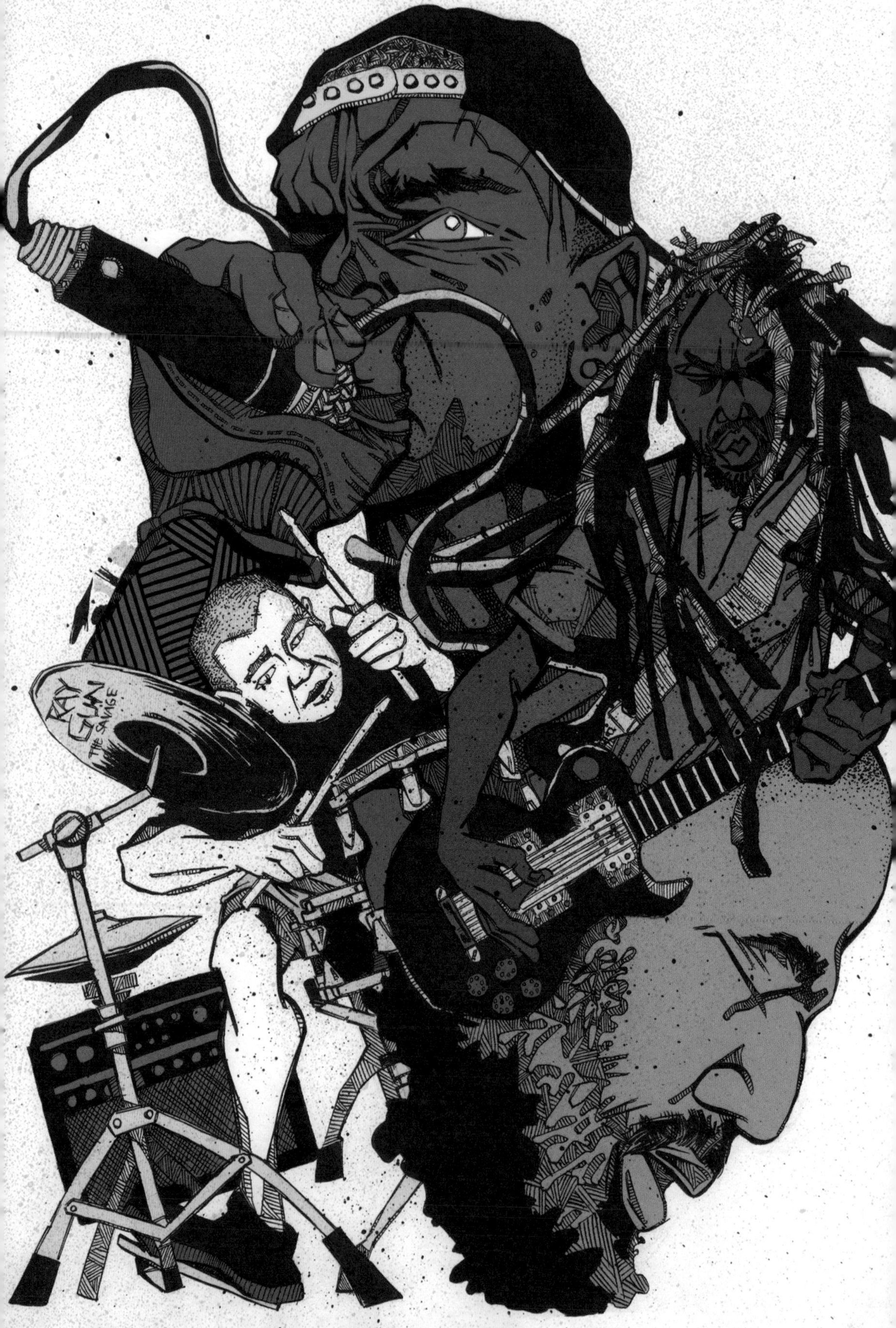

RAY GUN
THE SAVAGE

2011

KILLER OF SHEEP

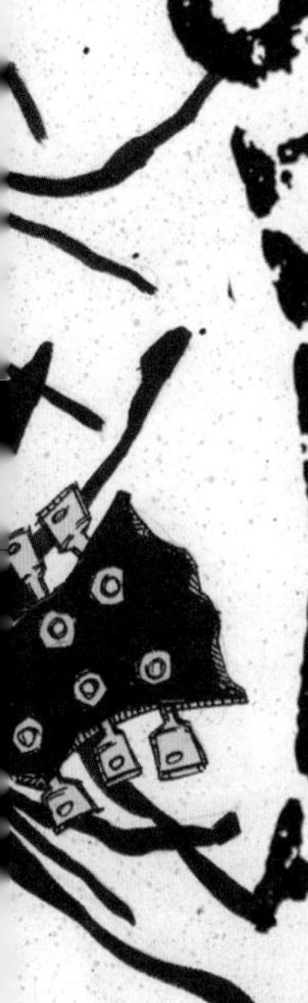

JORDAN MILES
BEATEN
FOR THE COLOR OF SKIN
HE WAS AN HONOR STUDENT
NO GUNS! NO DRUGS!
LISTEN!!!!
IN AMERICA
IT'S ILLEGAL
TO BE POOR!
THEY'RE GONNA LOCK US ALL UP
AND PUT
US IN PRISON
BEATEN FOR THE COLOR OF SKIN
BEATEN! BEATEN!
THEY RIPPED THAT BOYS HAIR OUT
WHY!!!!
IN AMERICA
IT'S ILLEGAL TO BE POOR!
THEY'RE GONNA ROUND US ALL UP AND
PUT US IN PRISON
.... AND THEY'RE COMING FOR YOU*

OYO ELLIS
OLLIE McCLELLEN
GREG MAIRS
CHRIS TRIP TREPAGNIER

* "Jordan Miles" by Killer of Sheep

PITTSBURGH

STEFAN BURNETT AKA MC RIDE IS A RAPPER WHO FRONTS THE BAND DEATH GRIPS, A THREE-PIECE BASED IN SACRAMENTO, CALIFORNIA. THEY RELEASED THEIR FIRST MIXTAPE "EXMILITARY" IN 2011. DEATH GRIPS ARE EXPERIMENTAL, AND CAN PRODUCE REPETITIOUS AND CYCLICAL BACKDROPS LACED WITH ERRATIC DISRUPTIVE STOPS AND MELODY CLASHES. IT'S A TAPESTRY OF FORCEFUL VOCALS, SYNTH, STACCATO, AND SAMPLES ON SAMPLES...FOR EXAMPLE: THEY GUILD TRACKS WITH FEEDBACK FROM BAD BRAINS, RIFFS FROM BLACK FLAG, ETHEREAL BJORK VOCAL CLIPS, AND EVEN AN EXPLOSIVE CRY OF VENUS WILLIAMS EXHALING ON THE COURT. LYRICS CAN SEEM STREAM-OF-CONSCIOUSNESS, DENSE WITH IMAGERY THAT MIGHT MAKE MORE SENSE TO EXPERIENCE AS MULTI-FACETED ABSTRACTIONS, RATHER THAN BE SHOVED INTO LINEAR TRANSLATIONS - THEY HAVE BEEN DESCRIBED AS SERVING THE ID.

RIDE SHUNS INTERVIEWS AND SHINES ON STAGE. THEIR COLLECTIVE CAN DISREGARD TRADITIONAL BEHAVIORAL CONVENTIONS WHEN IT COMES TO BUSINESS MODELS OR ADVERTISING; THEY'VE BEEN DROPPED FROM A MAJOR RECORD LABEL FOR RELEASING CONTRACTED MUSIC FOR FREE (WHEN THE LABEL ALLEGEDLY PUSHED A RELEASE DATE) THEY'VE IGNORED TOUR DATES, AND THEY'VE BEEN GENERALLY VAGUE & OPAQUE ON IF THEY EVEN REMAIN A BAND.

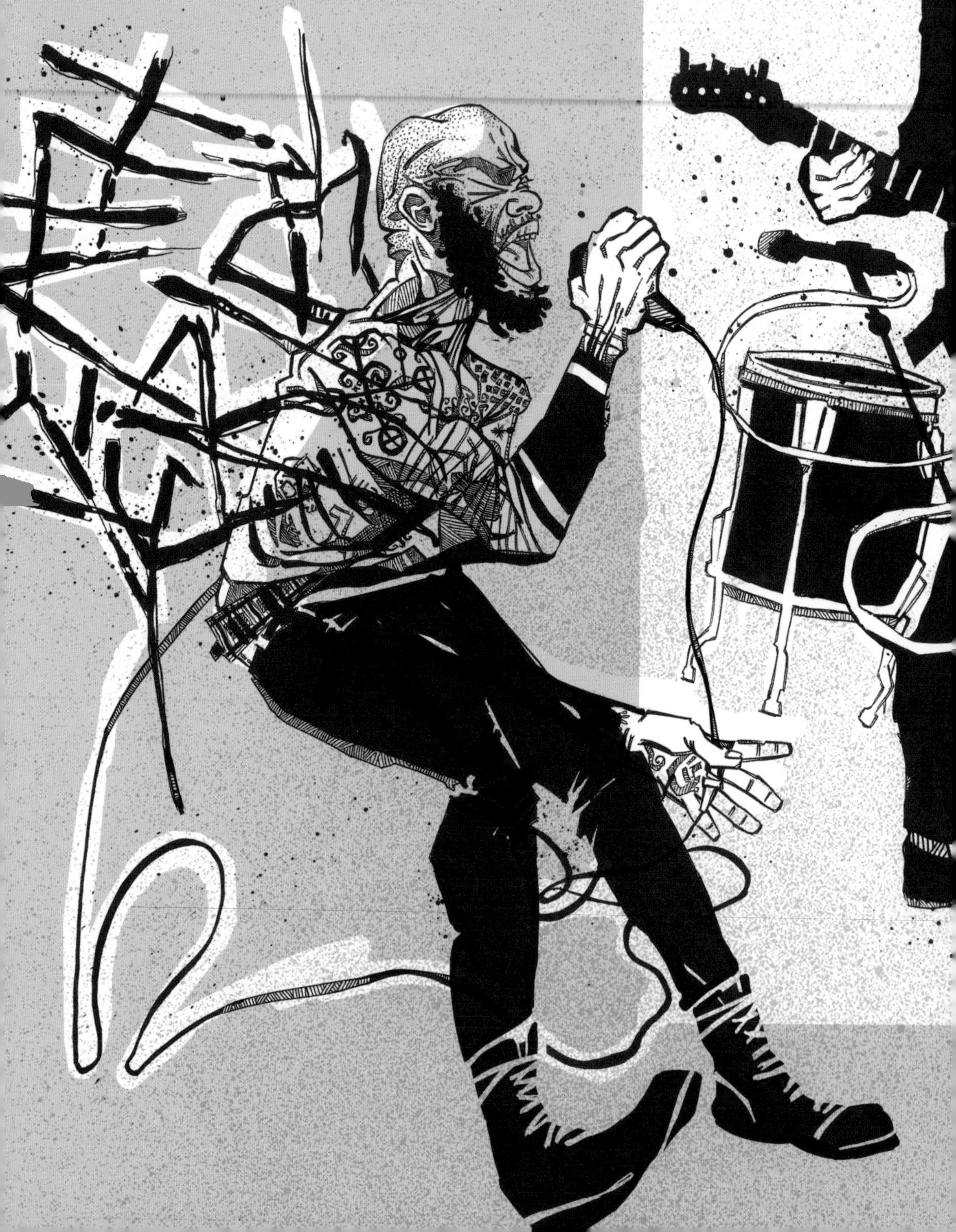

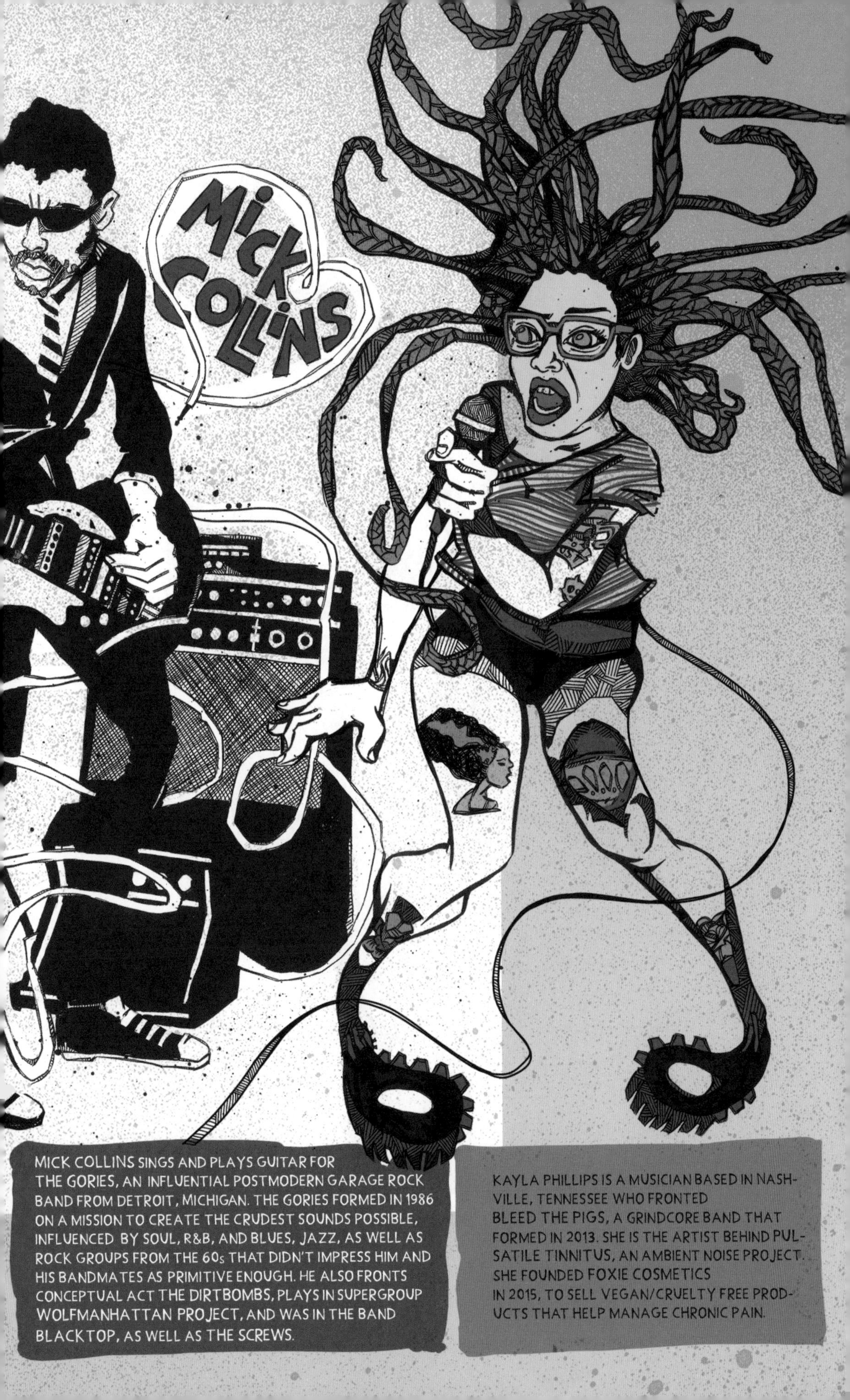
MICK COLLINS

MICK COLLINS SINGS AND PLAYS GUITAR FOR THE GORIES, AN INFLUENTIAL POSTMODERN GARAGE ROCK BAND FROM DETROIT, MICHIGAN. THE GORIES FORMED IN 1986 ON A MISSION TO CREATE THE CRUDEST SOUNDS POSSIBLE, INFLUENCED BY SOUL, R&B, AND BLUES, JAZZ, AS WELL AS ROCK GROUPS FROM THE 60s THAT DIDN'T IMPRESS HIM AND HIS BANDMATES AS PRIMITIVE ENOUGH. HE ALSO FRONTS CONCEPTUAL ACT THE DIRTBOMBS, PLAYS IN SUPERGROUP WOLFMANHATTAN PROJECT, AND WAS IN THE BAND BLACKTOP, AS WELL AS THE SCREWS.

KAYLA PHILLIPS IS A MUSICIAN BASED IN NASHVILLE, TENNESSEE WHO FRONTED BLEED THE PIGS, A GRINDCORE BAND THAT FORMED IN 2013. SHE IS THE ARTIST BEHIND PULSATILE TINNITUS, AN AMBIENT NOISE PROJECT. SHE FOUNDED FOXIE COSMETICS IN 2015, TO SELL VEGAN/CRUELTY FREE PRODUCTS THAT HELP MANAGE CHRONIC PAIN.

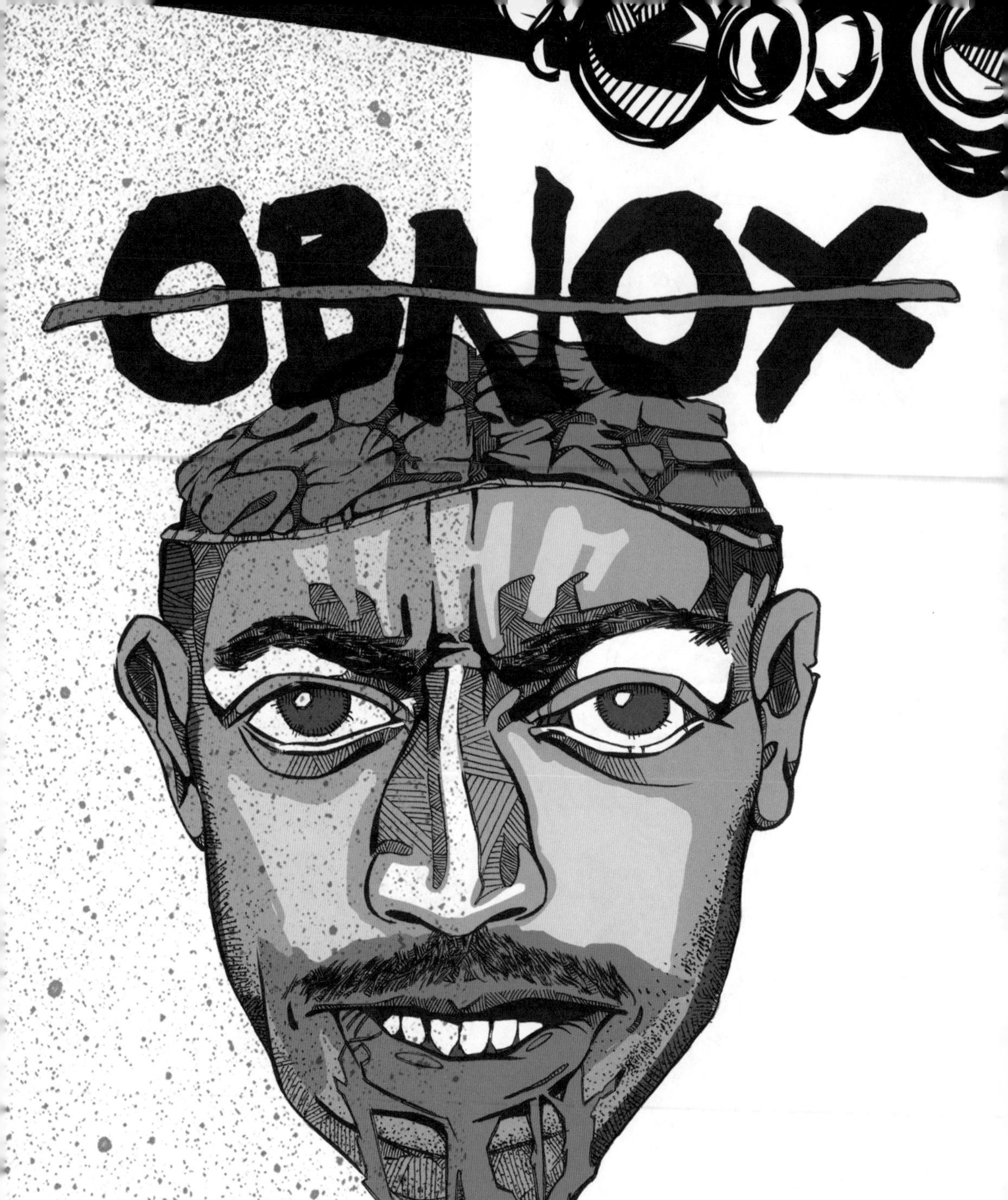
OBNOX
WHO

LAMONT "BIM" THOMAS BEGAN RECORDING IN 1995 AND HAS SINCE BECOME ONE OF THE MOST PROLIFIC VOICES IN ROCK 'N' ROLL. HIS MAIN MUSIC VEHICLE OBNOX HAS EXISTED SINCE 2011 IN CLEVELAND, AND HE'S DROPPED MULTIPLE RECORDS ALMOST EVERY YEAR SINCE ITS GENESIS. BIM HAS PLAYED IN THIS MOMENT IN BLACK HISTORY, PUFFY AREOLAS, AND BASSHOLES, AND RECORDED WITH CLEVELAND LEGENDS ROCKET FROM THE TOMBS. HE SINGS, DRUMS, AND PLAYS GUITAR, NORMALLY EXPERIMENTING WITH SOME COMBINATION OF HEAVY DISTORTION. HIS LAYERED WALLS OF SOUND REFERENCE ROCK, FUNK, JAZZ, SOUL, AND BLUES, AND BIM FREQUENTLY BRINGS IN OTHERS TO COLLABORATE.

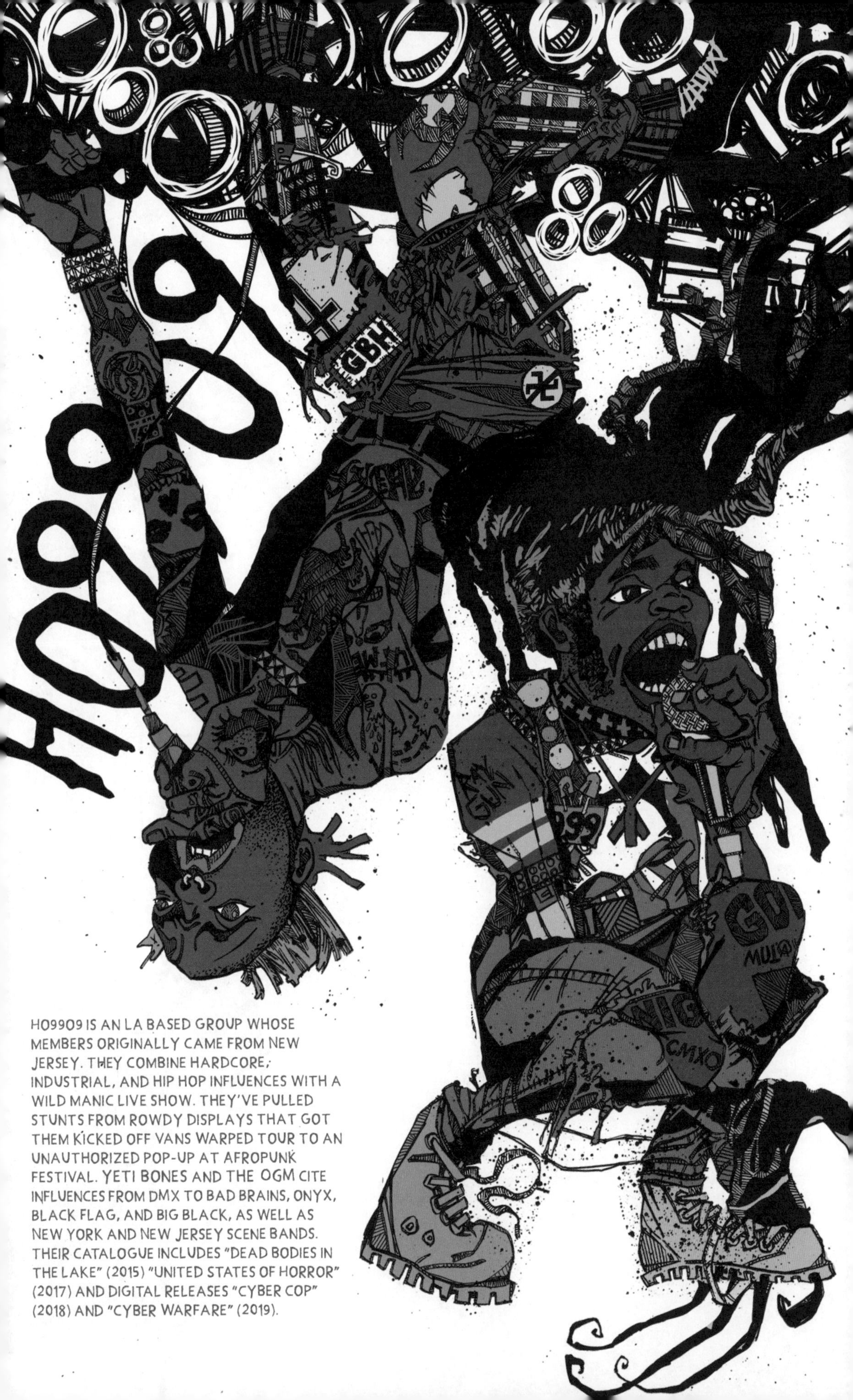
HO9909
GBH

HO9909 IS AN LA BASED GROUP WHOSE MEMBERS ORIGINALLY CAME FROM NEW JERSEY. THEY COMBINE HARDCORE, INDUSTRIAL, AND HIP HOP INFLUENCES WITH A WILD MANIC LIVE SHOW. THEY'VE PULLED STUNTS FROM ROWDY DISPLAYS THAT GOT THEM KICKED OFF VANS WARPED TOUR TO AN UNAUTHORIZED POP-UP AT AFROPUNK FESTIVAL. YETI BONES AND THE OGM CITE INFLUENCES FROM DMX TO BAD BRAINS, ONYX, BLACK FLAG, AND BIG BLACK, AS WELL AS NEW YORK AND NEW JERSEY SCENE BANDS. THEIR CATALOGUE INCLUDES "DEAD BODIES IN THE LAKE" (2015) "UNITED STATES OF HORROR" (2017) AND DIGITAL RELEASES "CYBER COP" (2018) AND "CYBER WARFARE" (2019).

BIG JOANIE

BIG JOANIE GUITARIST STEPHANIE PHILLIPS FOLLOWED A TRIED AND TRUE MUSICAL TRADITION WHEN SEARCHING FOR HER NEW BAND, A SIMPLE POSTED (IN THIS CASE DIGITALLY) ADVERT REQUESTING ATTENTION FROM THOSE WHO COULD TRUTHFULLY SHARE HER PERSPECTIVE AND WANT TO PLAY ABOUT IT. THE SCENE WAS TOO WHITE, AND SHE ENVISIONED BETTER REPRESENTATION. CHARDINE TAYLOR-STONE RESPONDED, CLAIMING DRUMS, AND SO IN 2013 BIG JOANIE WAS FORMED: A BLACK FEMINIST POST-PUNK GROUP WHO WERE VOCAL ABOUT THEIR POLITICS. KIERA COWARD-DEYELL JOINED AND EVENTUALLY DEPARTED, AND ESTELLA ADEYERI STARTED ON BASS TO ROUND OUT THEIR CURRENT LINEUP.

THE BAND SELF-DESCRIBES AS "LIKE THE RONETTES, FILTERED THROUGH 80s DIY AND RIOT GRRRL WITH A SPRINKLING OF DASHIKIS." THEIR FULL LENGTH "SISTAHS" WAS RELEASED IN 2018 ON THURSTON MOORE'S LABEL, THE DAYDREAM LIBRARY SERIES. THE BAND HAD RELEASED SEVERAL OTHER RECORDS, STARTING WITH THE "SISTAH PUNK" EP ON CASSETTE IN 2014.

BIG JOANIE STANDS UP FOR AND SUPPORTS LGBT RIGHTS, AND THEY ARE VERY INVOLVED WITH COMMUNITY. THEY ARE CONCERNED WITH THE EFFECTS OF WHITE SUPREMACY ON THE BLACK SENSE OF SELF AND EQUILIBRIUM, NAMING THEIR 2016 EP "CROOKED ROOM" TO REFERENCE POLITICAL COMMENTATOR MELISSA HARRIS-PERRY'S EXPLORATION OF THE CHALLENGES BLACK WOMEN FACE WITHIN CONDITIONS THAT ARE PURPOSEFULLY SET UP TO KEEP THEM UNBALANCED (SEE PERRY'S 2013 PUBLICATION SISTER CITIZEN). THE LYRICS TO "CROOKED ROOM" SWIRL AROUND A CLAUSTROPHOBIC BLUESY SHEPARD TONE OF A BASELINE, AND CONJURE UP A DREAM SEQUENCE WHERE THINGS MAKE JUST ENOUGH SENSE TO IMPLY ONE COULD GET TO A SOMEWHERE THAT ALWAYS REMAINS BEYOND REACH.

THE BAND COUNTERS SOCIETALLY ENFORCED DISTORTIONS OF BLACK SELF-IMAGE EVEN STARTING WITH THEIR NAME, A LOVING AND RESPECTFUL TRIBUTE TO STEPHANIE'S MOTHER JOAN. THE TERM "BIG" IS USED TO REFER TO A CARIBBEAN CONCEPT, WHERE THE BAND PLAYS WITH CONNOTATIONS OF THE AUTONOMOUS RIGHT TO TAKE UP SPACE: SOMETHING GENERALLY DISCOURAGED OR DENIED TO BLACK WOMEN/PEOPLE IN CERTAIN SPACES.

THE MEMBERS OF BIG JOANIE ALL WORK FOR CREATIVE AND POLITICAL LIBERATION OUTSIDE OF THE BAND. PHILLIPS STARTED DECOLONISE FEST IN LONDON FOR PUNK MUSICIANS OF COLOR, AND ALSO PUBLISHED "WHY SOLANGE MATTERS" IN 2021. TAYLOR-STONE IS A WRITER AND ACTIVIST, AND FOUNDED BLACK GIRL'S PICNIC AS WELL AS STOP RAINBOW RACISM. ADEYERI DJs AND ALSO WORKS WITH DECOLONISE FEST AND GIRLS ROCK LONDON.

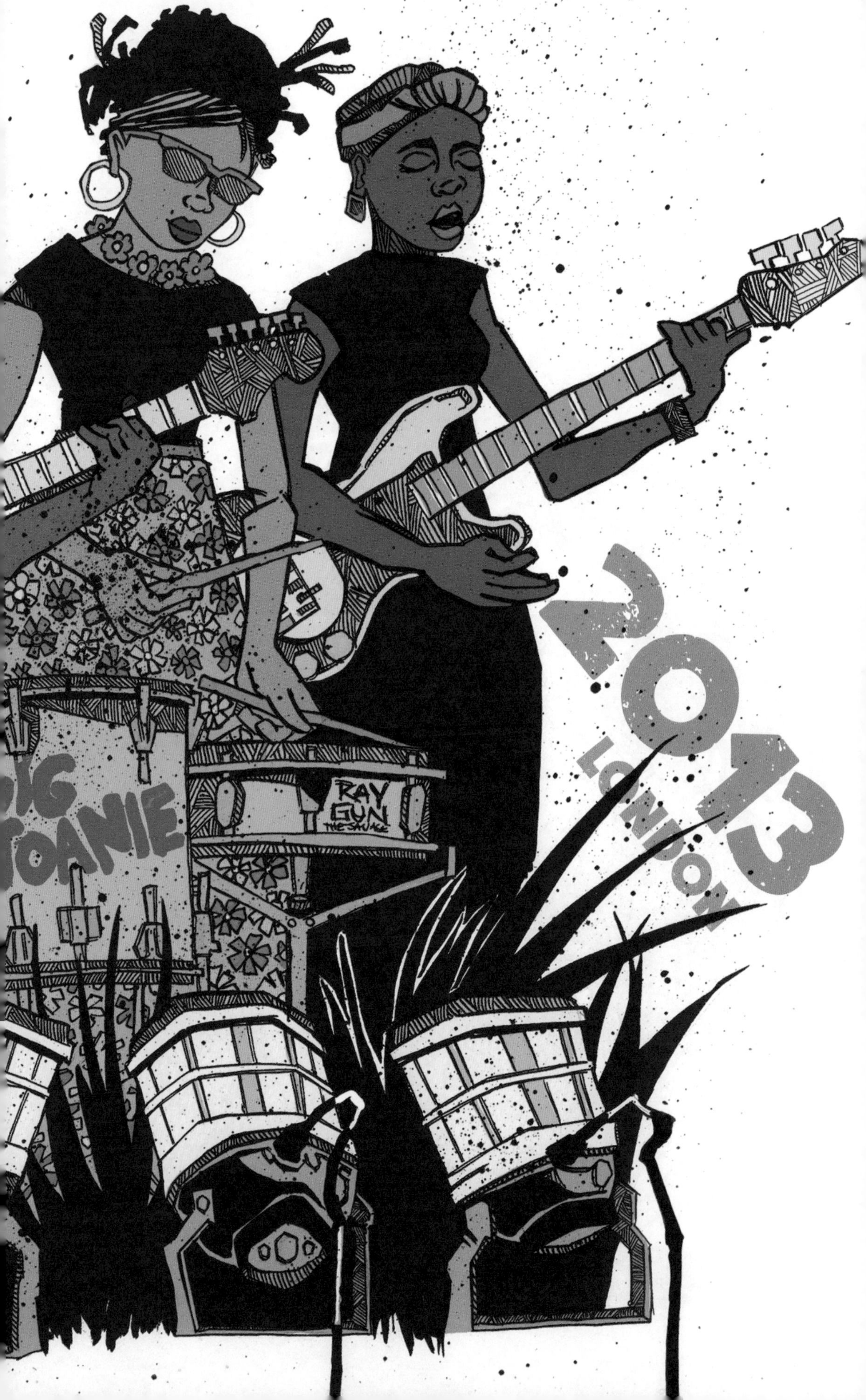
RAY GUN
THE SAVAGE
2013
LONDON

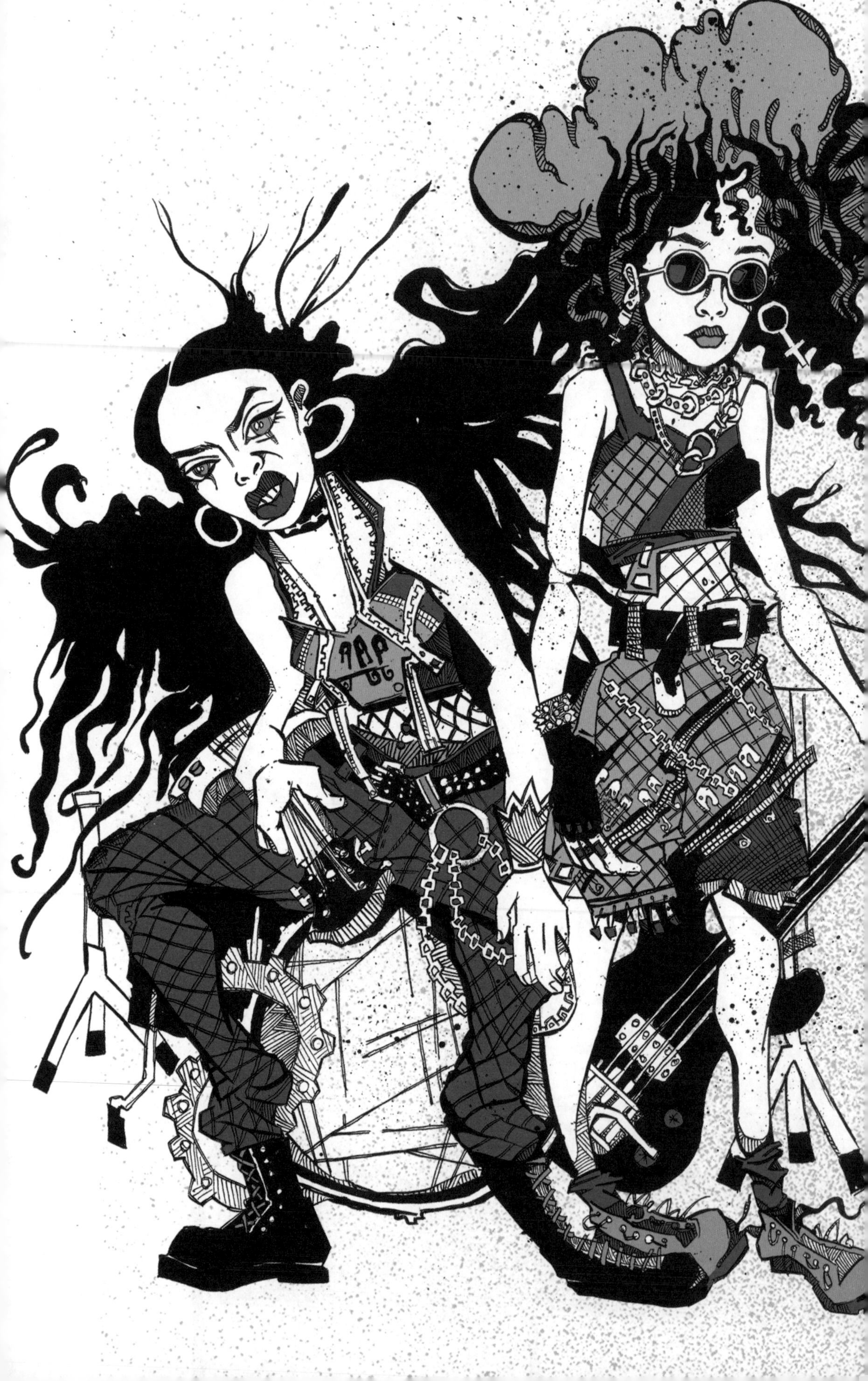

NOVA TWINS

NOVA TWINS IS A 2 PIECE FROM LONDON FEATURING AMY LOVE ON GUITAR AND GEORGIA SOUTH ON BASS, WITH BOTH CONTRIBUTING TO VOCALS. THEIR SOUND CROSSES GENRES, MESHING ROCK WITH 90s R&B AND SEWING IN PUNK, GRIME, AND RAP WITH RIVETING VOLUME PLAY AND ENERGY. A PROMINENT DISTORTED BASS EMANATES FROM GEORGIA AND HER HOLY PEDALBOARD, WHILE AMY'S AGITATED VOCALS CAN SWITCH FROM GROWLISHLY BREATHY WHISPERS TO FORCEFUL WINDING YELLING, AND LOTS IN BETWEEN; HER VOICE IS LIKE A SWISS ARMY KNIFE. THEY WERE FORMED IN 2014 AND RELEASED THEIR FIRST LP **WHO ARE THE GIRLS?** IN 2020 AFTER A STRING OF SINGLES AND EPs. OF ALL THE BANDS THAT I TELL PEOPLE ABOUT, THIS IS ONE THAT I ALWAYS HEAR BACK THAT PEOPLE DUG A LOT.

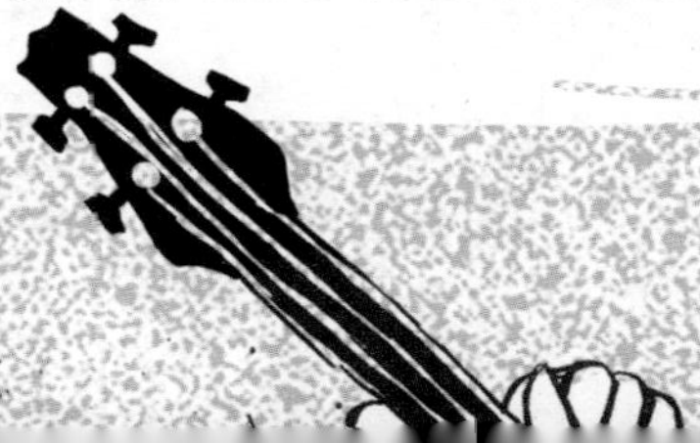

2014

LONDON

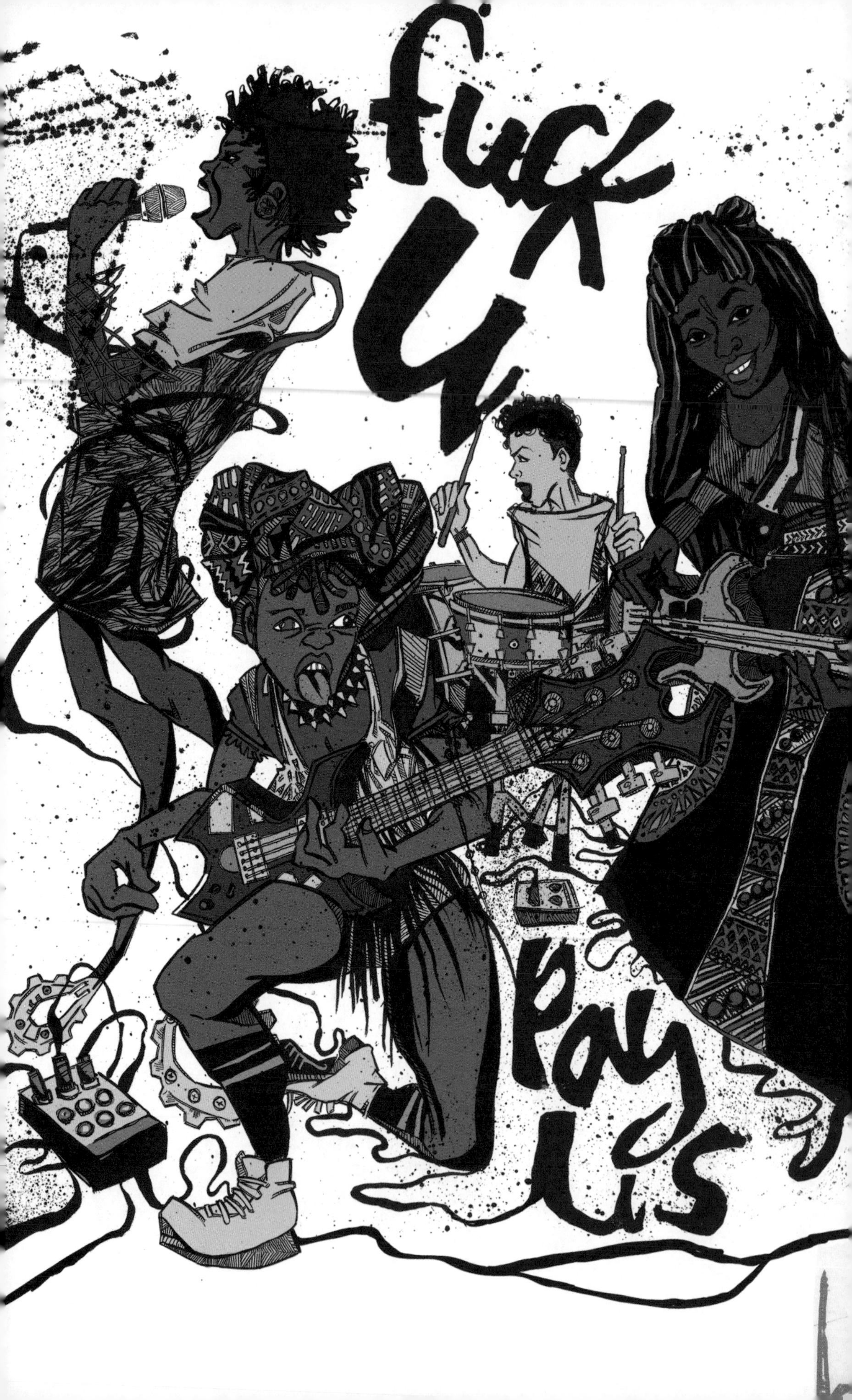
fuck U
pay us

FUPU

LOS ANGELES
2016

FUPU (FUCK U PAY US) IS A NO WAVE BAND THAT FORMED IN LOS ANGELES IN 2016, STARTED BY UHURU "THE UHURUVERSE" MOOR ON GUITAR AND SINGER JASMINE NYENDE. DRUMMER TIANNA NICOLE AND BASSIST AYOTUNDE OSAREME JOINED LATER (OSAREME HAS SINCE DEPARTED), AND CURRENTLY GUITARIST SUNNY WAR AND DRUMMER BAPARI ARE MEMBERS. THEIR SOUND IS INFORMED BY PUNK, BLUES, AND HIP HOP.

THEIR BAND NAME IS A NOD TO LIL' KIM LYRICS AND FUBU. IT IS ALSO A REFERENCE TO REPARATIONS: DEMANDING FORMAL MATERIAL COMPENSATION FROM THE UNITED STATES TO DESCENDANTS OF ENSLAVED PEOPLES, TO ATONE FOR STOLEN LIVES AND LABOR DURING AMERICAN CHATTEL SLAVERY. FUPU ENCOURAGES THEIR AUDIENCE TO TAKE CARE OF THE MUSICIANS IN THEIR COMMUNITY AND HELP FULFILL TANGIBLE ARTISTS' NEEDS, AS OPPOSED TO TREATING BANDS AS MERELY SPORADIC VEHICLES OF ENTERTAINMENT.

FUPU BANDMATES HOLD IDENTITIES THAT ARE COMBINATIONS OF QUEER, NON-BINARY, TRANS, AND FEMME, AND THEY TAKE CARE TO CULTIVATE SPACES TO BE COMFORTABLE FOR THOSE WITH SIMILAR IDENTITIES. THEY STAND UP FOR THEMSELVES AND OTHERS TO MAKE ROOM FOR CREATIVE DISCOURSE UNHAMPERED BY THOSE WHO INSIST ON WHITE CENTERED NARRATIVES. THEY USE THE RALLY CRY "BLACK FEMMES TO THE FRONT" TO HELP PEOPLE FEEL SAFER AND LESS INVISIBLE, AND TO COMBAT THE HISTORY OF MINORITIES BEING HARASSED AT SHOWS. THEY WISH FOR THEIR FANS TO BE ABLE TO HAVE FREE EXPRESSION, WITHOUT THE FEAR OF BEING RACIALLY (FALSELY) CATEGORIZED AS A THREAT TO OTHERS.

SONGS LIKE "DON'T TOUCH MY HAIR" AND "BURN YE OLD WHITE PATRIARCHY, BURN" CAN BE INSTANT BEACONS TO PEOPLE WHO MAY NOT NORMALLY HEAR THESE THINGS DISCUSSED IN A ROCK 'N' ROLL CONTEXT. "NAPPY BLACK PUSSY" ASSIGNS POWER TO TYPES OF HAIR THAT ARE MALIGNED BY SOME, WHILE ITS CHORUS OF "SUCK MY NAPPY BLACK PUSSY!" RESTRUCTURES THE STALWART 'FUCK YOU' SENTIMENT TO BE AIMED AT WHITE CONFORMITY POLITICS.

IN ADDITION TO THEIR STRONG MESSAGE OF REPARATIONS, FUPU EXPLORES RESPECT FOR ANCESTORS AND NATURAL THEMES, AS THEY SIMULTANEOUSLY CALL FOR AN ANTI-CARCERAL SYSTEM AND BLACK LIBERATION. AFTER A VIOLENT ATTACK FROM A WHITE SUPREMACIST DURING A 2017 UK TOUR, THEY ADDED SELF-DEFENSE READINESS TO THEIR MESSAGING.

YOU CAN FIND A RECORDING ONLINE: "LIVE AT CIELO GALLERY FOR MELANIN UNITY SHOW" (2017), AND THEY ARE IN THE MIDST OF PREPARING A NEW ALBUM NOW. THERE HAVE BEEN SOME HIATUS PERIODS, BUT MEMBERS STAY BUSY AND ACTIVE WITH INDIVIDUAL PURSUITS, AS WELL AS THE FUPU RADIO SHOW. THEY ARE ALSO FUNDRAISING FOR AN ARTIST RESIDENCE CALLED UHURU'S DREAM HOUSE: A HOME THAT IS A SAFE SHELTER FOR DISENFRANCHISED DISABLED BLACK TRANS, QUEER, AND INTERSEX PEOPLE.

NEGRO TERROR

COMMUNITY ACTIVIST AND MUSICIAN OMAR HIGGINS WANTED TO SHIFT A NARRATIVE THAT CLASSIFIED CERTAIN GENRES AS "WHITE MUSIC," AND IN 2015 HE RECRUITED DRUMMER RA'ID KHURSHEED AND GUITAR PLAYER RICO FIELDS TO FORM HARDCORE/OI BAND NEGRO TERROR.

IN ADDITION TO PLAYING SONGS DENOUNCING WRONGS LIKE ASSAULT AND THE UNITED STATES' LACK OF SUPPORT FOR MINORITIES, NEGRO TERROR DID A COUPLE OF IRONIC COVERS FROM A NEO-NAZI SKINHEAD BAND FROM THE 70s: SKREWDRIVER. NEGRO TERROR TOOK SKREWDRIVER'S ANTI-IMMIGRANT LYRICS AND WHITE FEAR CONTENT AND FLIPPED THEM OVER TO PAINT THE AMERICAN POLICE, NEO-NAZIS AND THE ALT-RIGHT AS THE REAL INTRUDERS. "VOICE OF MEMPHIS" (THIS VERSION OF SKREWDRIVER'S "VOICE OF BRITAIN") ADDS INSULT TO INJURY BY HAVING BETTER VOCAL STYLING AND MUSICIANSHIP, IN ADDITION TO FEATURING FINER LOOKING MEN THAN IAN STUART'S OLD BAND OF PASTY LILY WHITES! NEGRO TERROR HAS 2 RECORDINGS, "THE BOOTLEG" (2017) AND "VOICE OF MEMPHIS" (2019).

THE BAND WAS ALSO THE FOCUS OF A FULL LENGTH DOCUMENTARY BY JOHN RASH. AN ALBUM WAS RECORDED IN 2019: PARANOIA, THAT HAS NEVER BEEN RELEASED. IN APRIL OF 2019 HIGGINS PASSED AWAY. HE WAS AN INVOLVED AND LOVED MEMBER OF HIS SCENE, AND MANY SHOWED OUT TO HONOR HIM BY THROWING A MUSICAL BEALE STREET FUNERAL PROCESSION IN MEMPHIS ON HIS BEHALF.

PLEASE SEEK OUT NEGRO TERROR'S "VOICE OF MEMPHIS" MUSIC VIDEO! IT'S FILMED IN A LOCAL SKATE PARK, IT'S REALLY COOL, & IT'LL MAKE YOU FEEL REALLY PROUD.

RA'ID AND RICO HAVE CONTINUED ON AND ARE NOW PLAYING AS SEIZE AND DESIST, WITH PING D. ROSE.

PS. IF YOU WANT TO TALK ABOUT HOW SKREWDRIVER'S FIRST RECORD WASN'T RACIST: NO ONE CARES, AND DON'T KID YOURSELF ALL THAT NEO-NAZI STUFF DOESN'T JUST BUBBLE UP LIKE OUT OF THE BLUE.

MEMPHIS

2015

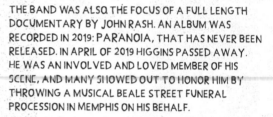

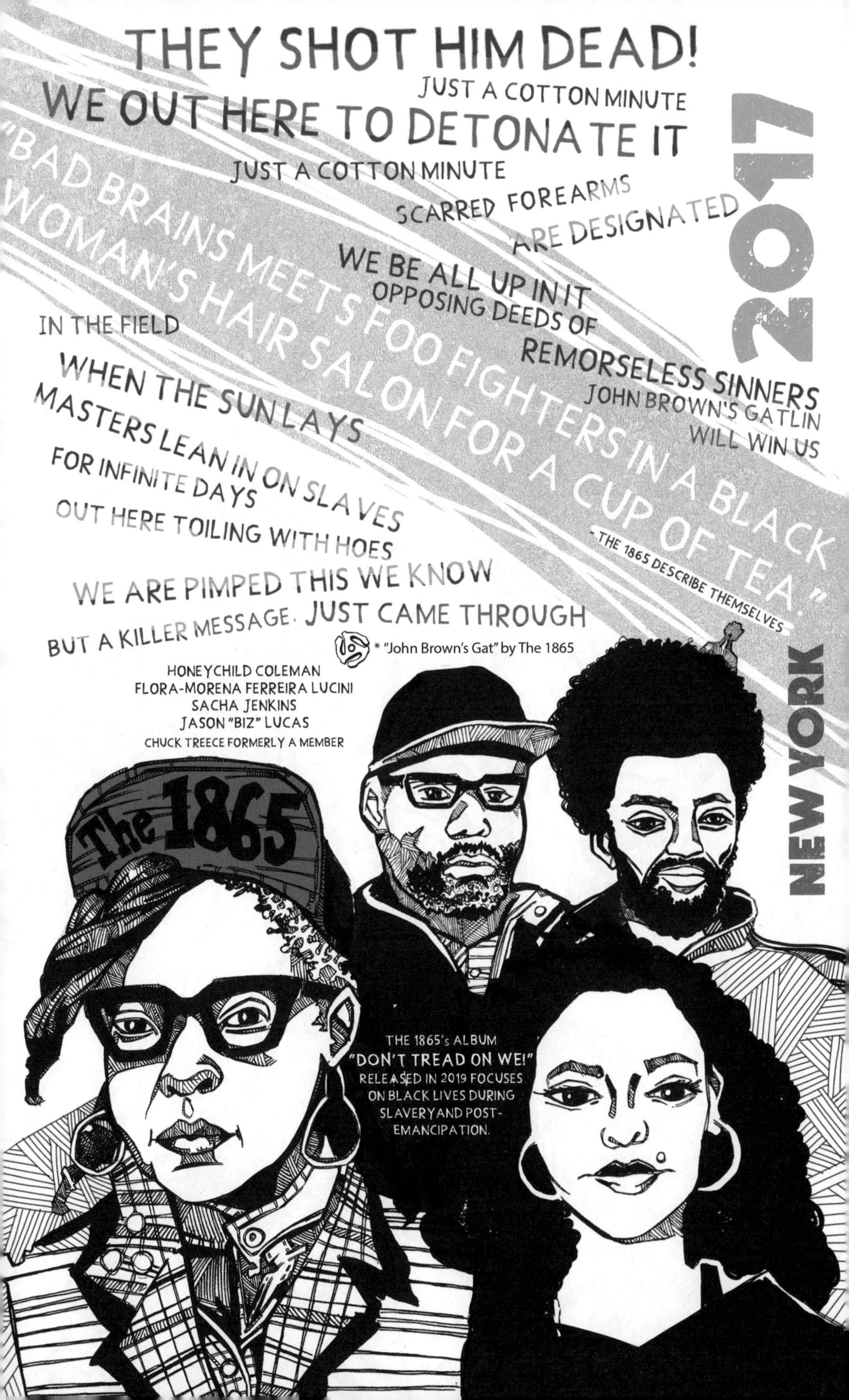
THEY SHOT HIM DEAD!
JUST A COTTON MINUTE
WE OUT HERE TO DETONATE IT
JUST A COTTON MINUTE
SCARRED FOREARMS
ARE DESIGNATED
WE BE ALL UP IN IT
OPPOSING DEEDS OF
REMORSELESS SINNERS
JOHN BROWN'S GATLIN
WILL WIN US
IN THE FIELD
WHEN THE SUN LAYS
MASTERS LEAN IN ON SLAVES
FOR INFINITE DAYS
OUT HERE TOILING WITH HOES
WE ARE PIMPED THIS WE KNOW
BUT A KILLER MESSAGE. JUST CAME THROUGH
* "John Brown's Gat" by The 1865
"BAD BRAINS MEETS FOO FIGHTERS IN A BLACK WOMAN'S HAIR SALON FOR A CUP OF TEA."
- THE 1865 DESCRIBE THEMSELVES
2017
NEW YORK
HONEYCHILD COLEMAN
FLORA-MORENA FERREIRA LUCINI
SACHA JENKINS
JASON "BIZ" LUCAS
CHUCK TREECE FORMERLY A MEMBER
The 1865
THE 1865's ALBUM
"DON'T TREAD ON WE!"
RELEASED IN 2019 FOCUSES
ON BLACK LIVES DURING
SLAVERY AND POST-
EMANCIPATION.

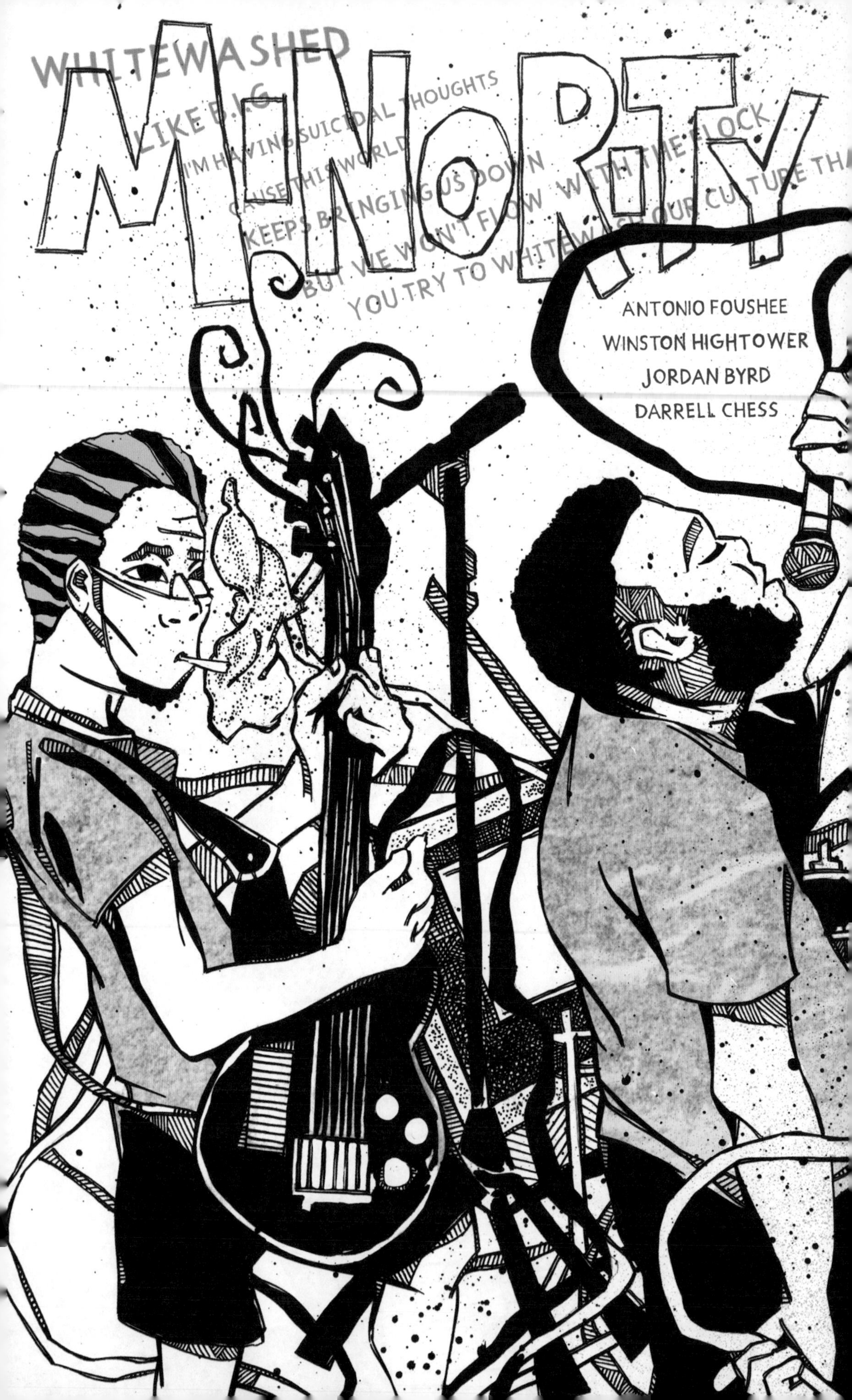
WHITEWASHED
MINORITY
LIKE B.I.G
I'M HAVING SUICIDAL THOUGHTS
CAUSE THIS WORLD
KEEPS BRINGING US DOWN
BUT WE WON'T FLOW WITH THE FLOCK
YOU TRY TO WHITEWASH OUR CULTURE THA
ANTONIO FOUSHEE
WINSTON HIGHTOWER
JORDAN BYRD
DARRELL CHESS

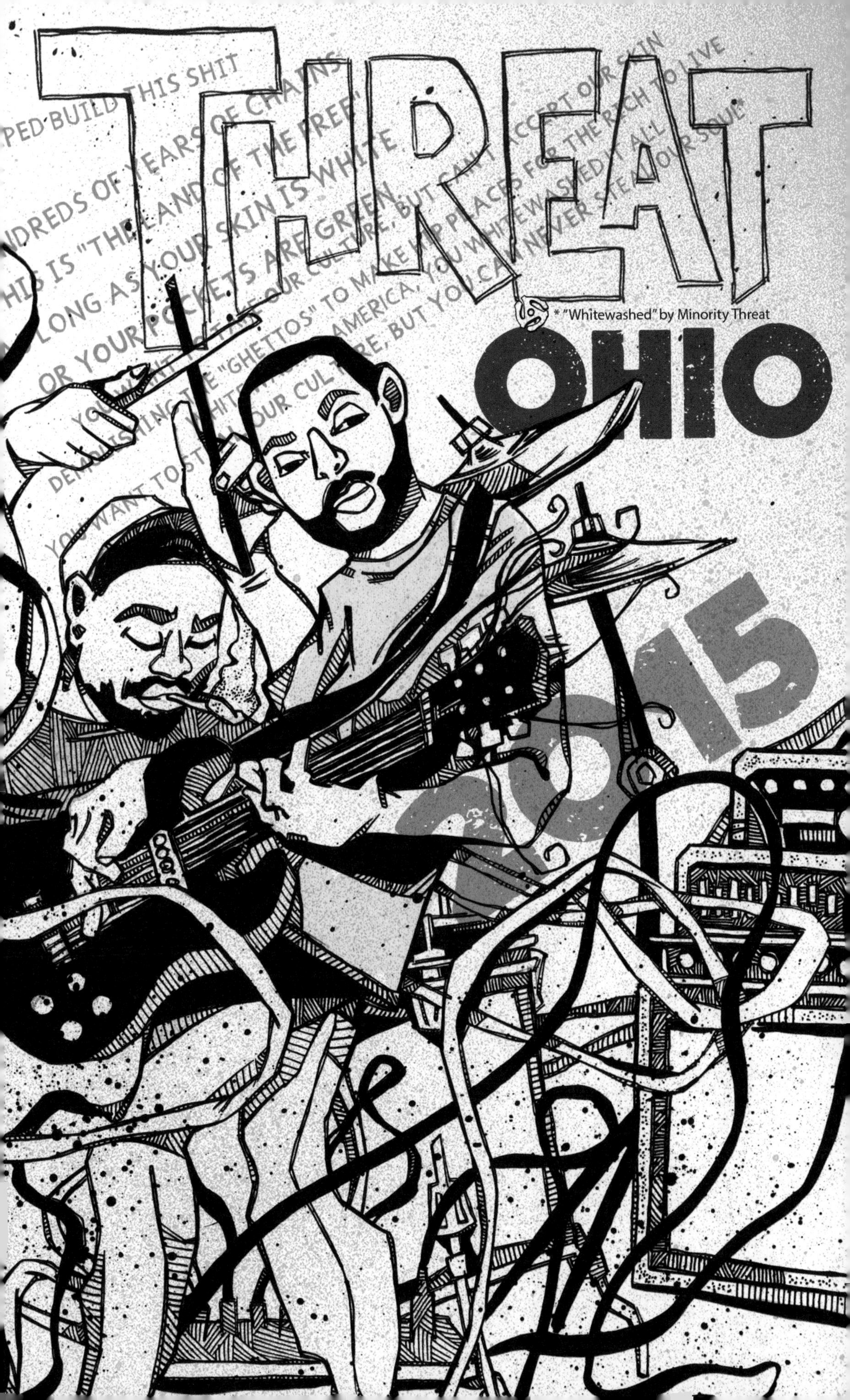

THREAT
PED BUILD THIS SHIT
NDREDS OF YEARS OF CHAINS
HIS IS "THE LAND OF THE FREE"
LONG AS YOUR SKIN IS WHITE
OR YOUR POCKETS ARE GREEN
* "Whitewashed" by Minority Threat
OHIO
2015

This is a researched and well-loved artifact, and it is about real people. I attempted to craft honest interpretations of source materials when illustrating and building first-person conversation, but any sequential art or first-person texts are merely heartfelt attempts at reenactments, as I wasn't there when any of the conversations or actions within occurred. A bibliography is included, but we apologize for errors in advance and if notified, we can update any misprints in further printings.

ROSETTA THARPE
Wald, Gayle F. Shout, Sister, Shout! The Untold Story of Rock-And-Roll Trailblazer Sister Rosetta Tharpe. Boston: Beacon Press, 2007.

The Godmother of Rock & Roll: Sister Rosetta Tharpe, directed by Mick Csaky (2011; United Kingdom: BBC). Accessed on YouTube. Uploaded to Claudia Assef channel on March 7, 2019. https://youtu.be/FKK_EQ4pj9A

Anderson, William C. "THE BLACK WOMAN AND THE BLACK CHURCH THAT BIRTHED ROCK MUSIC." MTV, March 6, 2016. https://www.mtv.com/news/2794983/sister-rosetta-tharpe-black-woman-rock-music/

DEATH
Rubin, Mike. "This Band Was Punk Before Punk Was Punk." The New York Times, March 12, 2009. https://www.nytimes.com/2009/03/15/arts/music/15rubi.html

"Interview: Death, Detroit proto-punk rebels." Red Bull Music Academy, January 12, 2016. https://daily.redbullmusicacademy.com/2016/01/death-interview

PURE HELL
George, Cassidy. "The forgotten story of Pure Hell, America's first black punk band." Dazed. August 8, 2018. https://www.dazeddigital.com/music/article/40942/1/pure-hell-first-black-american-punk-band-history

Pure Hell, interview with Kenny Gordon, Preston Morris, Lenny Boles. Accessed on YouTube. Uploaded to Keith Niedzielski channel on December 3, 2008. https://youtu.be/hdxMwNNRA2o

Dawes, Layna. "Q&A with Pure Hell on Innovation, Evolution and the '70s Punk Scene." Decibel Magazine. August 11, 2014. https://www.decibelmagazine.com/2014/08/11/q-a-with-pure-hell-on-innova-tion-evolution-and-the-70s-punk-scene/

"Pure Hell." In the Red Records. April 12, 2017. https://intheredrecords.com/blogs/news/pure-hell

DON LETTS
Letts, Don. "'Dem crazy baldheads are my mates.'" The Guardian. October 23, 2001. https://www.theguardian.com/culture/2001/oct/24/artsfeatures4

SHOWstudio: Stussy - Talking Punk with Don Letts and John Ingham, SHOWstudio. Accessed on YouTube. Uploaded to SHOWstudio channel on November 8, 2013. https://youtu.be/CmNle0qSLuE

Samadder, Rhik. Letts, Don. "Don Letts: 'Punk is not mohawks and safety pins. It's an attitude and a spirit.'" The Guardian. February 7, 2015. https://www.theguard-ian.com/music/2015/feb/07/don-letts-this-much-i-know

BLACK DEATH
Swift, M. "Black Death: The First All-Black Heavy Metal Band." Black Then. November 29, 2021. https://blackthen.com/black-death-first-black-heavy-metal-band/

BAD BRAINS
Minsker, Evan. "Sid McCray, Original Bad Brains Singer, Has Died." Pitchfork. September 13, 2020. https://pitchfork.com/news/sid-mccray-original-bad-brains-singer-has-died/

POLY STYRENE
Sweeting, Adam. "Poly Styrene Obituary." The Guardian. April 26, 2011. https://www.theguardian.com/music/2011/apr/26/poly-styrene-obituary

PAT SMEAR
Collected issues. Slash Magazine. published and edited by Steve Samiof and Melanie Nissen. San Francisco, CA, 1877-1980. PDF downloaded from www.circulationzero.com.

Collected issues. Damage Magazine. Edited by Brad Lapin. San Francisco, CA, Damaged Goods Company, 1979-1981. PDF downloaded from www.circulationzero.com.

KARLA MADDOG
Afro-Punk, directed by James Spooner (2003; United States). Accessed on YouTube. Uploaded to AFROPUNK channel on March 20, 2013. https://youtu.be/fanQHFAxXH0

Karla Maddog. "KARLA MADDOG: THIS IS YOUR PUNK ROCK LIFE! (OR, HOW THE MASQUE WAS WON BY THE MADDOG." personal website. http://maddogx_78.tripod.com/madbio.html

ESG
Trammell, Matthew. "ESG's Otherworldly Sound." The New Yorker, February 23, 2018. https://www.newyorker.com/magazine/2018/03/05/esgs-otherworldly-sound

Steiner, Melissa Rakshana. "It's Music That Makes You Dance" - ESG Interviewed." The Quietus. September 7th, 2015. https://thequietus.com/articles/18707-esg-interview

Kot, Greg "ESG turned 'accident' into music history." Chicago Tribune. May 24, 2018. https://www.chicagotribune.com/entertainment/music/ct-ott-esg-interview-0525-story.html

PAULINE BLACK
Interview: Pauline Black (The Selecter). PRS for Music. Accessed on YouTube. Uploaded to PRS for Music channel on October 11, 2015. https://youtu.be/ZbVdKtXG6s4

"How Skinheads Transformed From An Inclusive Youth Movement Into A Racist Hate Group." All That's Interesting. October 4, 2021. https://allthatsinteresting.com/skinheads-history

Under The Influence: 2 Tone Ska. Noisy. Accessed on YouTube. Uploaded to Noisy channel on May 11, 2015. https://youtu.be/AGV6i8kiOHw

Byrne, Eugene. "St Pauls 1980: The causes and consequences of a night of violent clashes." Bristol Live. April 2, 2020. https://www.bristolpost.co.uk/news/bristol-news/st-pauls-1980-causes-consequences-4010112

Gourley, Robert. "2-TONE MEMORIES: PAULINE BLACK AND THE SELECTER." Please Kill Me. July 4, 2019. https://pleasekillme.com/pauline-black-selecter/

BASQUIAT
Holman, Michael. "New York Stories: Michael Holman." Red Bull Music Academy, May 26, 2013. https://daily.redbullmusicacademy.com/2013/05/new-york-stories-michael-holman

JEAN BEAUVOIR
Leigh, Nathan. "Afropunk Interview: Jean Beauvoir Is Original Punk." AFROPUNK. September 7, 2018. https://afropunk.com/2018/09/afropunk-interview-jean-beauvoir-original-punk/

"Jean Beauvoir." Nine Lives Entertainment. https://nine-lives-entertainment.com/artist/152/Jean_Beauvoir/en

BIG JOANIE
Samways, Gemma. "REBEL GIRLS: BIG JOANIE." DIY Mag. November 25, 2020
https://diymag.com/2020/11/25/rebel-girls-big-joanie-november-2020-interview

"We're like The Ronettes filtered through '80s DIY and riot grrrl." Punktuation!
Magazine. September 1, 2020.
https://www.punktuationmag.com/big-joanie-were-like-the-ronettes-filtered-
through-80s-diy-and-riot-grrrl/

"BLACK FEMINIST PUNK GROUP BIG JOANIE RELEASES NEW SINGLE INSPIRED BY
MELISSA HARRIS-PERRY." Super Selected. June 17, 2016.
https://www.superselected.com/black-feminist-punk-group-big-joanie-releases-
new-single-inspired-by-melissa-harris-perry/

FUPU
Thomas-Hansard, Artemis. "FUPU: the battle of LA." Dazed Digital. December 15,
2017. https://www.dazeddigital.com/music/article/30307/1/fuck-u-pay-us-band-
punk-la-activism

Gale, Nikita. "Omniaudience (Side One)." Triple Canopy. December 12, 2018.
https://www.canopycanopycanopy.com/contents/omniaudience--side-one?sub-
=gale--nyende-conversation

Cardoza, Kerry. "The Punk "Radiance and Rage" of Fuck U Pay Us." Bandcamp. November 20, 2017. https://daily.bandcamp.com/features/fupu-feature

HANIF ABDURIQUIB
Communication via email with Hanif Abdurraqib, March 5, 2019.

KILLER OF SHEEP
Killer of Sheep. "Jordan Miles/Gasolina." Track 3 on Scorned. 2017, Taaang! Records.
Bandcamp. https://killerofsheep1.bandcamp.com/track/jordan-miles-gasoline

BOBBY PORTER
O'Driscoll, Bill. "Pittsburgh loses a singular voice: Bobby Porter." Pittsburgh City
Paper. November 18, 2010. https://www.pghcitypaper.com/pittsburgh/pitts-
burgh-loses-a-singular-voice-bobby-porter/Content?oid=1380560

Leraci, Ron. "Bobby Porter." Old Mon Music. October 30, 2010. http://oldmonmu-
sic.blogspot.com/2010/10/bobby-porter.html

DEATH GRIPS
"Death Grips decided not to show up to Lollapalooza, their aftershow, or Osheaga,
cancel Webster Hall & other dates." Brooklyn Vegan. August 4, 2013.
https://www.brooklynvegan.com/death-grips-dec/

"Death Grips Dropped by Epic Records." Rolling Stone. November, 2, 2012.
https://www.rollingstone.com/music/music-news/death-grips-dropped-by-epic-
records-183771/

Indiana, Jake. "ARE DEATH GRIPS THE MOST IMPORTANT HIP-HOP ACT OF THE
DECADE?" High Snobriety. 2018. https://www.highsnobiety.com/p/death-grips-
hip-hop-history/

MICK COLLINS
Episode 2: The Gories. Detroit Punks. directed by Dawn Gifford Engle and Eliza-
beth Holloway (April 20, 2015; United States). Accessed on YouTube. Uploaded to
Detroit Punks channel on June 1, 2015. https://youtu.be/F_M-sDhllil

KAYLA PHILLIPS
"PULSATILE TINNITUS - Kayla from Bleed the Pigs/Foxie Cosmetics." Hear She Roars. May 13, 2019.
https://www.hearsheroars.com/post/pulsatile-tinnitus-kayla-from-bleed-the-pigs-foxie-cosmetics

OBNOX
Communication via email with Lamont Thomas, February 2019.

HO99O9
Watson, Elijah. "Ho99o9 is Climbing The Ranks Of Hard Rock — One Chaotic Show At a Time." Okay Player. Accessed May 18, 2022. https://www.okayplayer.com/originals/ho99o9-live-show-interview.html

Hill, John. "Ho99o9 Call Out 'Huge Emos' With 'Rape Charges' at Punk Fest." CLRVYNT. May 9, 2017.
https://clrvynt.com/ho99o9-interview/

NEGRO TERROR
Mehr, Bob. "Memphis punk and reggae musician Omar Higgins dead at age 37." Memphis Commercial Appeal. April 21, 2019. https://www.commercialappeal.com/story/news/2019/04/21/omar-higgins-dead-memphis-punk-reggae-musician-age-37/3533631002/

Zaillian, Charlie. "Negro Terror Expands the Horizons of Hardcore Punk." Nashville Scene. January 10, 2019.
https://www.nashvillescene.com/music/features/negro-terror-expands-the-horizons-of-hardcore-punk/article_6ae062ab-357f-533f-81e2-9f4041fbc9f0.html

THE 1865
Communication via email with Honeychild Coleman, May 18, 2022.

The 1865. Don't Tread on We. Mass Appeal, 2019, Bandcamp. https://the1865.bandcamp.com/album/dont-tread-on-we

MINORITY THREAT
Minority Threat. "Whitewashed." Track 4 on Culture Control. Self released, 2015, Bandcamp.
https://minoritythreat.bandcamp.com/track/whitewashed-2

Death photo by Tammy Hackney (page 8, 9) referenced.

Pure Hell photos, Welfare Records (cover, page 10) referenced with permission.

Bad Brains photo by Steven Hanner (page 19) referenced with permission.

Black Death photo by Anastasia Pantsios (page 21) referenced with permission.

Arthur Lee photo by Andy Willsher (page 39) referenced with permission.

Bobby Porter photo by unknown photographer (page 41) referenced.

Kayla Phillips photo by Rosie Richeson (page 47) referenced with permission.

Lamont Thomas photo by Byron Miller (page 48) referenced with permission.

Honeychild photo by Ed Marshall (page 57) referenced with permission.

THE SECRET HISTORY OF BLACK PUNK

Shades of the initially esoteric punk rock movements that hit their crescendo in the 70s can be seen everywhere in typical society now... in near perpetual dream-colored hair, in mass produced (and consumed) pre-distressed fashions from online stores bearing safety pins, chains, studs and possibly a flirtation with rude sentiment, et cetera, ad nauseum.

But in spite of this oversaturation, being Black and punk can still - present day, and in certain circles - be met with wonder and derision. Being a Black weirdo or outcast doesn't always guarantee welcomed entry into the still overwhelmingly white (tho ever evolving) punk scenes. If you do meander in, you might not like what you find there.

Bands that scream about equality and acceptance and denounce the police state and racism may still tokenize you and ask you to accept brutal to casual racism, penalizing you if you don't. You might actually be seen as a threat to the harmony of an insular scene of people if you suggest effective direct anti-racist action. You might be pressured into playing the role of the quiet or safe i.e. unopinionated minority to stay safe.

You'll find the ancient white punk proverb "Have you ever heard of Bad Brains?" a condescending inquiry masked as a bumbling attempt to relate to the Black punk who is treated as an outsider and novelty.

"Why are you so angry?" an especially puzzling denouncement in rooms full of slam dancing and aggressive, high voltage lyrics containing strong convictions and challenges.

Sometimes there is a flat out: "You don't ACT Black" or "Whoa, but you're BLACK." Equally alienating sides of the same coin, one that implies that liking punk rock culture is a rejection of inherent Blackness, and one that expresses a hesitation to accept that a Black person would stray from the "approved" Black genres of music: rap (or funk) or rap. There is that final battle cry from the children of Elvis, a desperate attempt to own and gatekeep: "Punk is WHITE."

Racism, whitewashing, and microaggressions won't be solved by breaking up homogeneity in the punk scene. And the truth is that many Black musicians don't actually really give a shit about staying within the boundaries that confine punk to the rigid genre that some bands and scene purveyors had corralled it into directly after the first wave. The best case scenario here is that having to seek any sort of acceptance or acknowledgement from an overly white punk scene (via record contracts or social ones) will become obsolete, merely a hangover for earlier punks of color with no choice but to conform to certain standards at risk of being left behind.

I think I write all of the above to get it out of my system. I want to acknowledge it and then get on with the telling of stories. I do believe that it needs to be acknowledged, and I believe in trying to provide tools to counteract widely accepted yet annoyingly outdated ideas and narratives. But I don't think it's anyone's job to have to defend Black punk to anyone, or to be continuously contextualizing it to outrun white narratives. All I can do is document and add another testament to the record.

And there is a growing record now: documentaries, essays, zines, social media accounts, publications, and fests dedicated to celebrating Black punk today, as well as new bands being formed in the underground all the time...

#uptheblackpunks ok thank you, 4 now I'm done.
- Raeghan